EAST RENFREWSHIRE

09195548

KT-417-240

EA 6-6-15

29 JUN 2015

22 AUG 2015

25 SEP 2015

16 OCT 2015

- 1 NOV 2015

- 5 JUN 2018

18 SEP 2018

21 MAY 2019

18 JUN 2019

Return this item by the last date shown.
Items may be renewed by telephone or at
www.eastrenfrewshire.gov.uk/libraries

East
Renfrewshire
COUNCIL

| | | | |
|---|---|---|---|
| Barrhead: | 0141 577 3518 | Mearns: | 0141 577 4979 |
| Busby: | 0141 577 4971 | Neilston: | 0141 577 4981 |
| Clarkston: | 0141 577 4972 | Netherlee: | 0141 637 5102 |
| Eaglesham: | 0141 577 3932 | Thornliebank: | 0141 577 4983 |
| Giffnock: | 0141 577 4976 | Uplawmoor: | 01505 850564 |

# HOW BAKING WORKS

# HOW

# BAKING

JAMES MORTON

# WORKS

EBURY
PRESS

10 9 8 7 6 5 4 3 2 1

EBURY PRESS, AN IMPRINT OF EBURY PUBLISHING,
20 VAUXHALL BRIDGE ROAD,
LONDON, SW1V 2SA

EBURY PRESS IS PART OF THE PENGUIN RANDOM HOUSE GROUP OF COMPANIES
WHOSE ADDRESSES CAN BE FOUND AT GLOBAL.PENGUINRANDOMHOUSE.COM

PHOTOGRAPHY © ANDY SEWELL 2015
COPYRIGHT © JAMES MORTON 2015

JAMES MORTON HAS ASSERTED HIS RIGHT TO BE IDENTIFIED AS THE AUTHOR OF
THIS WORK IN ACCORDANCE WITH THE COPYRIGHT, DESIGNS AND PATENTS ACT
1988

FIRST PUBLISHED BY EBURY PRESS IN 2015

WWW.EBURYPUBLISHING.CO.UK

A CIP CATALOGUE RECORD FOR THIS BOOK IS AVAILABLE FROM THE BRITISH LIBRARY

PHOTOGRAPHY: ANDY SEWELL
DESIGN: WILL WEBB
STYLIST: LAURA FYFE
COPY EDITOR: RACHEL MALIG

ISBN: 9780091959906

COLOUR REPRODUCTION BY ALTAIMAGE
PRINTED AND BOUND IN CHINA BY C&C OFFSET PRINTING CO., LTD

PENGUIN RANDOM HOUSE IS COMMITTED TO A SUSTAINABLE FUTURE FOR
OUR BUSINESS, OUR READERS AND OUR PLANET. THIS BOOK IS MADE FROM
FOREST STEWARDSHIP COUNCIL® CERTIFIED PAPER.

# HOW THIS WORKS

## HOW THIS WORKS

This book is for the unpretentious. Everything is simple. Everything is direct. There's as little useless flowery language as I could muster. I'll remove all the steps you don't need and tell you why you don't need them. I bought every ingredient from my local, medium-sized supermarket.

This book is for everyone who thinks baking should be fun.

This book is for people who *want* to chuck things in and see what happens. The basics are broken down and explained. Not just the 'How', but the 'Why', so you'll know exactly what you can change and substitute and switch and what you can't. If anything ever goes wrong, or has ever gone wrong before, we'll look at what it could be and why it happened and what you can do to stop it ever happening again. This book is for anyone who wants answers. Maybe you've tried to make a macaron and it turned out tasting like porky fish, as mine once did. Or maybe you've had a disaster with choux pastry that somehow turned out both soggy and dry, as mine has done many times. Here are all the answers (I think). And if I've missed anything, catch me on Twitter and I will find out for you. I'm @bakingjames.

Here's to getting it right first time.

## HOW TO USE THE BOOK

Like with my first book, *Brilliant Bread*, I've refused to conform to the standard 100 or so recipes (of which about three are useful or original) that litter most texts. This project is simply about how to make an awesome cake. Or meringue. Or pie. Or tart. I'll guide you through the basics, then stress what works and what doesn't.

The recipes are *mere suggestions*.

Go through this book without baking a single one of them and I'll still be delighted (especially if you paid for it). They are designed to help you improve upon your own favourites and to form the foundations of your own creations. If you've got time, please start by taking a look through these first chapters on ingredients and equipment. Especially the ingredients. I believe that knowing a bit about their characters and what you can do to them is imperative to understanding what happens when you combine them in a recipe. Then you'll find all the skills and techniques that I'll reference again and again in the recipes: the custards and the ganaches. As well as the routine stuff, like how best to whip cream, use a piping bag or make jam. Then we begin baking. At the start of each chapter, you'll find a guide on how to master that particular style, broken down into the following sections.

## 1. THE IDEAL

This is the necessary opening of each chapter, for it first gives you an idea of what to look for in your final bake. My philosophy on cooking and baking (and pretty much everything creative) is that it doesn't matter which method you use, it's your final result that matters. Although a rigid approach could be said to discourage individuality, it shows you what is expected. I baked a tarte Tatin with a soggy bottom for years before realising it wasn't actually supposed to congeal when I chewed it.

## 2. STEP BY STEP

This section guides you through the processes involved in the creation of a particular dish, stopping short of baking. I will stress how to carry out each step and then break up each one further into tiny wee baby steps. Then I'll explain *why* we're doing what we're doing. The deeper you understand something, the less likely you are to forget it.

Sometimes these will be referenced in the other recipes within the chapter. You'll find little variation between bakes – the principles and the pitfalls are the same for each one.

## 3. THE BAKE

The bake itself. I hope the theme across all these sections is one of reiteration. The range of baking times and temperatures is tiny, if you look closely. Pretty much all the recipes in this book are baked within 40 degrees of one another. And the thermostats on many ovens are out by far more than that.

Baking will require a bit of tinkering and getting to know your own oven. Mine has more than 50 degrees of variation, front to back and top to bottom, and it can still turn out a pretty perfect batch of macarons. It just takes a little getting used to.

## 4. VARIATIONS

This is a short list of variations to the base recipe and when to use them. These are usually just wee additions or recommended replacements, but they can make a big difference. This list is not exhaustive, but it should give you  plenty to try. Exponentially more if you combine them.

## 5. SUBSTITUTIONS

When I was canvassing opinion about ideas for this book, this was the section most people requested. If you've got plain flour but don't have any self-raising, what can you do? That's an easy one for some – but what about eggs? Butter? Are you a coeliac? Dairy intolerant? Most of the substitutes that can be made without significant detraction are covered in these sections.

## 6. STORAGE

It helps to know how long you can store baking and in what state. You'd be amazed at how many bakes freeze excellently. Most store well in their component parts, then when you're nearly ready to serve you can assemble without having to do any of that annoying stuff involving an oven.

## 7. TROUBLESHOOTING

The stuff that went wrong and what you can do about it. I'd be surprised if your complaint isn't listed in these sections, though I've omitted such classic quandaries as: 'My cake is burnt after forgetting it for an hour'.  As a quick aside, the answer to nearly every timing-related problem is to set a timer on your mobile phone.

## 8. RECIPES

These are ingredient amalgamations that I have tried and succeeded with. If you want examples of some variations to the given recipe, there are usually a few here too. The rest is up to you.

I sincerely hope you have fun with them. If you're used to following recipes to the letter, this might be a bit strange. Be reckless. If you've read all the rest, you'll know that switching that egg you're missing for a little milk probably won't make any noticeable difference.

## A LITTLE ABOUT ME

I'm James. I was once on a show called *The Great British Bake Off*. Being on that show has afforded me the opportunity to write about what I like writing about. Like almost all of my living costs, this mostly relates to food and drink.

I'm also a medical student. In fact, by the time these words are in print I should be a fledgling doctor or thereabouts. It has often been observed that all this cake-evangelism might make me a busier clinician in later life. We'll see, I say.

I like to bake. A lot. And I suppose the aforementioned hospital-surfing is why I like things to be right. I like justice and I like evidence. Even amongst my most pedantic of colleagues, I'm referred to as many things far too obscene to print in relation to my insistence on high-quality, peer-reviewed meta-analyses in mundane discussion.

My approach is one of scepticism. Apply this to baking and you soon realise that most of what everyone has said for hundreds of years is either misleading or false. My spare time is spent trying to decipher the falsehoods from the truths, then writing them down in a book. Some fools even decided to publish them. Twice.

FOREBAKE

# FOREBAKE

Reading this chapter isn't strictly necessary, but I'd recommend it above most others. It will explain a little about the background of each ingredient, leading to a more comprehensive understanding of *how baking works*.

The equipment list is short, and that is intentional. You don't need much to get baking well. And the quality of your oven is never, ever an excuse. You should see the state of mine.

# INGREDIENTS

## FLOUR

Flour is ground-up wheat. For the most part it's white, meaning that the outer shell of the wheat's kernels (the 'bran') has been sieved out on an industrial scale and then what little is left is bleached until it looks like mounds of ground-up diamonds. (Although I promised not to be pretentious, I think this simile does my eternal love for pure white flour justice.)

Check out the back of a packet of plain flour. It isn't just starch, but a complex mix of everything a potential wheat plant might need to grow from. This includes some haphazard proteins (8–10%), some sugar, a bit of fibrous content (even in white flour) and an array of things more biological: interesting enzymes, spores and even plenty of living bacteria and yeasts.

Gluten (see Latin: *glue*) is part of the protein content. It's an amalgamation of two proteins: gliadin and glutenin. These stick together to form a matrix that gives most baking its structure. Even when we want as little gluten formed as possible, such as in cakes or pastry, it still provides the backbone that stops them sinking into a mush. It can be developed further by beating or kneading, but if too prevalent it gives tough or chewy cakes and cardboard-like pastry. Gluten should be avoided by those with coeliac disease, but virtually everyone else can enjoy it without fear of repercussion.

White flour comes in three types in the UK: strong, plain and self-raising. Strong flour has loads of gluten-forming proteins in it and is used to make bread, croissants and puff pastry. It will absorb more water than plain flour. Plain flour is low-gluten flour designed for most baking – anything except bread and laminated pastries. Self-raising flour is plain flour with added baking powder – up to about 5% of the weight. It can always be substituted for plain flour and baking powder (1 teaspoon per 100g) or vice versa. Raising agents do go off though, so make sure your self-raising flour or baking powder is in date.

Wholewheat flours are to be avoided in most cakes, biscuits and other sweet treats. If your diet is lacking in fibre, there are plenty of better places to get it without ruining everyone else's fun. Wholewheat can add a nice complexity of flavour and texture in savoury bakes, as can all the other interesting flours of varying nutritional worth.

## RAISING AGENT

The raising agent is an adjunct ingredient to help make your bakes rise, but it is not the only thing that will cause expansion. It is possible to have a poor rise using plenty of raising agent and a good one through purely mechanical means. I believe it is important to understand why.

When stuff heats up, it expands. If there are any bubbles of air inside your mix, such as those created by whisking whole eggs, folding in egg whites or creaming butter and sugar, they'll expand in the oven to make it rise. Mixing incorporates air, but this has to be finely balanced: any mixing after the flour has been added will cause a tough final product due to the overdevelopment of gluten. This is why all whisking and creaming is usually done before the flour is added. Equally, if there is any carbon dioxide dissolved in your mix (produced by yeast or by a raising agent), this escapes when it heats up because it can't dissolve as well in hot mixes. And where does it go? Most of it goes into the tiny bubbles that either you've created intentionally or that happen to be there anyway. If there aren't enough bubbles, your texture will tend to be quite uneven and any gas that can't be supported will escape into the oven.

The two most common raising agents are bicarbonate of soda and baking powder. The first (the same thing as baking soda) is a weak alkaline called sodium bicarbonate, which when heated turns into a stronger alkaline called sodium carbonate, releasing carbon dioxide. The problem is that the resulting sodium carbonate can taste a bit soapy.

Baking powder gets round this problem by mixing sodium bicarbonate with a weak acid, usually cream of tartar (for the geeks, potassium hydrogen tartrate). The alkaline and acid react together when mixed and heated, creating twice the amount of carbon dioxide than bicarbonate of soda and leaving little or no undesirable baking soda taste.

## FAT

Do I need to explain the real reason for the use of fat within baking? I think we all know that fat of any kind is pretty awesome. Many of us worry about the effect of fat upon our health, but it's important to remember that the type of fat we eat is important. All fats are high in calories, but they do play a necessary role in all of our diets, so please do enjoy them in moderation.

Oils, especially sunflower oil, contain plenty of mono- and poly-unsaturated fats and will lower cholesterol. Even butter, seen as the worst by many, isn't as bad as you might think. All those overhyped saturated fats aren't the ones you should be worried about. It's the 'trans' or 'hydrogenated' fats that you've got to watch – these are implicated in a staggering array of diseases. Check 'healthy' or 'low-fat' margarines and ready-meals for trans fats in abundance.

In baking, fat has several roles above and beyond flavour. The first is in the creaming. This is the mixing of fat with sugar. The sugar tears through the fat, trapping lots of tiny bubbles of air within fat droplets by simple mechanics. These expand when heated to make your bake rise.

Fat also makes mixes and pastries 'short'. This describes the crumbly texture associated with a high fat content and is why pastry is described as 'shorter' when it's made with more butter. Shorter mixes are more easily broken apart, softer and tend to coat the mouth for a more pleasurable texture. This all happens because the fat slows the formation of gluten, weakening the matrix. This is why many breads are usually kneaded before adding the butter.

Butter comes in unsalted and salted form. Both are fine, but the salt content varies wildly so it's difficult to give you an idea for substitutions. I tend to use salted butter for the simplicity of not adding any extra salt, so just add a wee pinch of salt if all you've got is unsalted.

*N.B. In recipes that require a tin to be greased, you will need a little extra butter i.e. more than the weight given in the recipe.*

## SUGAR

Table sugars (refined and unrefined sucrose) come from sugar cane or beets. You can buy them as caster (finely ground, white), granulated (less finely ground, white), icing (superfine grind, white) and an array of less refined brown sugars. The brown colour is due to the presence of varying amounts of treacle (molasses) within the crystals, giving them moisture. This contributes to the softness of many brown sugars. Treacle, after all, is a by-product of sugar refining.

Sugar is used primarily for the sweetness for which we worship baking, but it has a few other flourishes up its sleeve.

Sugar aids the formation of air bubbles when creamed with the fat – those little crystals have sharp edges, so rip through butter when beating, causing loads of little tears. The more sugar, the more moist your bakes, too, because sugar attracts water in exactly the same way as salt draws it in. This is why you can use sugar as a preservative – any bugs that might think about spoiling your jam or chutney get most of their water content sucked out of them as soon as they land.

Sugar doesn't make pastries shorter like butter, but it does have a big effect on their structure. The gliadin and glutenin that usually bind together to form gluten will, in the presence of lots of sugar, readily bind to the sugar instead. This gives a weaker structure and thus a more snappy, easily broken product.

When it comes to taste, sugar is far more than just sweet. Sugar changes considerably when hot, and especially above 160°C. The first type of reaction that occurs is caramelisation – this is essentially gradual burning (for the geeks, pyrolysis) to leave varying amounts of free carbon. If done correctly, this gives caramel baskets and spun sugar their brown colour; or a black colour if boiled for too long.

When you heat sugar, it melts in a similar way as ice to water, but that's not the only chemical change. It also breaks apart. When you make a caramel, you're making what's called an 'invert sugar syrup'. This consists not of *sucrose*, as table sugar at room temperature, but of its component parts: *glucose* and *fructose*.

Many bakers will have experienced the dreaded caramel crystallisation (see page 27). This happens when your caramel spontaneously turns back to sucrose, usually through agitation (stirring) or the addition of sucrose causing a chain reaction. Don't fret, though. Acid, as well as heat, causes the inverse reaction, so adding some lemon juice and a little bit of time will save any crystallised caramel. Hallelujah.

## SALT

Salt makes things taste nice. It's a fact. That's why everyone seems to be bringing out a salted caramel, salted ice-cream, salted banana, salted everything. You know what I call salted caramel? Caramel. I am of the camp that adds a touch of salt to most bakes because of its blatant flavour-enhancing wondrousness. A great way to boost the flavour of anything without the worry of going overboard is to replace unsalted butter with salted butter.

Worried about your blood pressure? Please don't sacrifice on flavour by adding less salt: just have a smaller piece. Sadly, we can't have everything.

## EGGS

Eggs are the backbone to many a baked good. You can buy various different sizes and types; all I can recommend is to go for medium eggs, unless otherwise specified. From free-range hens. A medium egg will give you 45–50 grams of liquid egg (it's often worth weighing if you're unsure), which is right for most standard cake and meringue ratios. The free-range bit is far more about the flavour and colour the happy hens somehow imbue into their yolks than any ethical position on my part.

Eggs are used for several reasons. First, and perhaps foremost, are their remarkable air-capturing properties. When beaten, eggs froth up. This is due to the high protein content of the egg white. Usually these proteins, called albumins, are all curled and tortuous, but they flatten out with vigorous beating with a whisk or by chemical (acidic) addition. The introduction of air by the whisk both aids the unfurling of the proteins and allows them to form into little bubbles, which give cakes and meringues their lightness. The introduction of fat hampers the bubble-making process markedly, for the flattened out proteins form an emulsion with the fats rather than with the air.

The proteins also unfurl and expand with higher temperatures, increasing the leavening effects of eggs (this is why you should not use eggs straight from the fridge). They then permanently bind at high temperatures in the oven, causing them to lose their fluidity, and setting the structure of the bake in place. Fresher egg whites contain more of the correct and intact proteins and are a bit more acidic than older ones, meaning they should give a more stable structure.

Egg yolks, on the other hand, are extremely useful in forming emulsions. This means that they act to dissolve fat in water (or vice versa), in much the same way as washing-up liquid. This is mainly due to the two-sided chemical structure of one particular protein present: lecithin. One side binds to fat, the other to water. Simple. Practically, this acts to bind mixtures together and retain moistness within cakes. Cakes made solely with egg whites tend to be dry and cloying.

## NUTS

I thought I'd include a wee section on nuts in baking, as they are a very important adjunct and a core ingredient in many of my recipes. And yes, I hear the pedants yell, I'm lumping in those that aren't truly nuts here too (like almonds and peanuts). As far as baking is concerned, they're all fairly similar. They all have an extremely high fat content and thus similar applications. The main area in which they differ is their flavour.

Nuts can be toasted in advance of use in order to enhance their savoury flavour and to release their oils – this will also prevent them sinking to the bottom of mixtures during the bake. Note that toasted nuts have a shorter shelf life; indeed, nuts don't last forever – you're talking six months maximum before you'll start to notice a sour tinge.

Nuts can be used to make a low-carbohydrate, gluten-free flour substitute to great effect (see the torte chapter, pages 115–129). They simply act as a filler in this role, as they don't contain any proteins with the characteristics of gluten. To make a nut flour, simply chop until dust-like in a food processor. Indeed, it is always better to chop rather than crush nuts, as the crushing action squeezes out many of the oils and can mean you end up with a spreadable nut butter rather than ground nut flour. This is the same reason why coffee aficionados use burr grinders rather than blade grinders – the crushing action of the former squishes out all the hard-to-reach oil-soluble flavour compounds.

## CHOCOLATE

Chocolate seems to have a kind of magic surrounding it, but it's simple enough. It's made from dried fermented cocoa beans that are found inside the fruit of the cocoa tree. These hard beans are made into chocolate like peanuts are made into peanut butter – they're roasted, dehusked and crushed together, albeit in a slightly more convoluted way. I once had the pleasure of eating ripe cocoa fruit and found it delicious; ironically we just tossed the hard beans into the bush.

The final stage in chocolate production is tempering, in which the size of the cocoa butter crystals is controlled by changing the temperature subtly. Chocolate can take six different crystal forms, and each has different properties, including melting point. By melting all the crystals and then reducing the temperature so that only certain crystals can form, chocolate is tempered. The crystals formed between the temperatures of 28–33°C have the best shine and snap. Reckless tempering leaves chocolate matt, rough and crumbly.

Care should always be taken when melting chocolate, but a full temper does not need to be carried out regularly at home. This is because shop-bought chocolate has already been tempered expertly. My own trick is to melt the chocolate very slowly until it has only just melted, then 'seed' it with finely chopped solid chocolate, so the crystals in the melted chocolate line up to match the crystals of the seeded chocolate. See pages 28–30 for my guide to tempering chocolate.

Don't mix your chocolate too much; just like in butter, the fats can form little air bubbles that will affect the texture. And not in a good way like a Wispa or Aero. And never, ever let your chocolate near water lest you disrupt its finely balanced texture completely. Even storing your chocolate in too humid an environment causes the surface to 'bloom' (creating those white marks) as its sugars dissolve in the moist air.

## FRUIT

One question should always be on your mind when baking with fruit: do I *need* to incorporate it into the bake itself, or can I get away with adding it afterwards? Fruit has a very high moisture content, which can cause all kinds of sogginess if used too liberally, especially within the uncontrolled environment of the oven. Equally, many of the more subtle flavour compounds within fruit are volatile and liable to escape or become tainted with heat. It all depends on what you're going for, but you should consider whether adding the fruit at the start actually brings anything to the dish.

An easy example might be a chocolate brownie. I could add strawberries into the mixture, but should I? They'd have to be some pretty astounding strawberries for their flavour to compete with the intense chocolate after a blasting. They're likely to shrink to nothing and release so much water that the bake takes 20 minutes longer to cook and still ends up damp. A no brainer: bake the brownies plain or with nuts, slice and then cover in chopped strawberries to serve. Or choose another more baking-friendly fruit: raspberries, for example.

## ESSENCES & EXTRACTS

This is a difficult one for me. On the one hand, I applaud the use of any ingredient that can add new flavours to a bake. But can I condone the use of artificial E-numbers, improvers and chemicals?

An 'extract' is a liquid made by soaking the extracted ingredient in some kind of solvent (usually alcohol). You can make your own (very high-quality) vanilla extract, for example, by soaking three or four split vanilla pods in a half bottle of vodka. Extracts tend to be natural, high-quality affairs that extract the true flavour compounds from an ingredient.

An 'essence', however, tends to be a man-made, wholly synthetic phenomenon. For example, vanilla essence tends to be made from a synthesised, cheaper compound called 'vanillin'. This doesn't happen to have an E-number, but others do.

Should you even consider the use of these essences? Definitely, I'd say. If it improves the bake, please use it. Compounds such as vanillin do occur naturally too, and essences can be used to complement natural flavours if used correctly. I don't specify any essences in the recipes of this book, though, so it's up to you. Wherever I do call for a natural extract, please don't substitute with an essence. Remember they are two different things.

# ESSENTIAL EQUIPMENT

## OVEN
You need an oven in which to bake things. It could be a gas oven, a standard electric oven or a fan oven, but if you've got a wee portable or a massive oil-fired affair, they'll be fine too. In short, the cost and quality does not matter; what matters is that you know your own oven. Many of the temperatures I give will need to be tweaked to suit you. One way to be more sure is to invest in that wonderful invention, the oven thermometer (though even these aren't nearly as accurate as everyone says they are . . . )

## ELECTRIC SCALES
Though vintage balance or bright-red mechanical scales might look pretty, they're useless nowadays. What's best for baking are flat, electronic scales. You can place your bowl on top, zero it, and weigh all your ingredients straight into your mixing bowl. Look for ones that are accurate to within 1g, and that have a reasonable capacity (anything 2kg or over).

## WHISK
Whisks are for whisking: fast beating that incorporates significant air or quickly gets rid of lumps in wet mixtures. Whisks cannot be used on stiff, hard mixes or dry doughs. They are extremely efficient at developing gluten, so should not be used in the final stages of cake-making. A handheld electric whisk can be used for everything from combining to beating to whisking, but make sure the beaters are totally clean (not greasy) before use.

## BIG SPOON
Wooden spoons, or any hard spoons without flex, are perfect for general mixing and beating, when a whisk would be too flimsy or stuff would get stuck inside the wires (for example when creaming butter and sugar). You should ideally use a large metal spoon for folding. The thin sides and large surface area help to cut efficiently to the bottom of the mix without smooshing those delicate air bubbles you've worked so hard to incorporate.

## BOWL

The choice of bowl is up to you. Plastic and silicon are easy to scrape clean, and any doughs or mixes will fall out easily. However, if used for whipping egg whites, they must be cleaned thoroughly with soap, rinsed and then rubbed with lemon juice and dried before use; their microscopically rough surface collects fats, which will ruin meringues and light mixes. Choose glass or ceramic and you avoid this problem, but these are heavy and break easily. Stainless steel is my first choice – I believe it's the best of all worlds.

## KNIFE

Always 'knife', never 'knives'. You don't need to spend a large sum on an elaborate knife set and block; take whatever your total budget is and buy a single, good chef's knife (probably Japanese), as well as something to hone or sharpen it: a steel or stone. If you invest in one chef's knife, you'll find yourself using it for everything from veg to meat to fish to bread, and it will be far safer than any blunt alternative.

## SPATULA/SCRAPER

Spatulas are useful for removing the last remnants of mixtures from bowls. You don't need one, but they reduce waste significantly. A compromise is buying a dough scraper – these are more rigid than spatulas and have all manner of bread-baking uses (see my first book, *Brilliant Bread*), as well as being efficient scoops and bowl-cleaners. They are especially good for filling piping bags.

## BAKING PAPER

Baking paper is my favourite consumable – it's well worth stocking up on. Forget the old (admittedly cheaper) greaseproof paper; baking paper is coated with silicone to make it non-stick. It is also far more effective than those reusable silicone sheets that many now tout. You can cut it to size, but I tend to just rip it and stuff it into whatever tin I'm using. That way, I rarely need to grease. Only turn to the uncoated stuff when setting caramel, for the silicon sticks and ruins your shiny finish.

## TINS

The size of the tins you'll need will depend on what you want to bake. You can get most of (nay all) the tins you could ever want at your local sizeable supermarket. Paying extra for non-stick if available is probably not worth doing – you'll be covering most of them with epic quantities of baking paper and what little is left deserves a good coating of grease.

My list of recommended tins is short (unless you're wanting to get into novelty cake decorating, and I strongly recommend you don't). I'd go for one or two large baking trays (as big as fits your oven). For cakes, a couple of 7 or 8-inch sandwich cake tins, a 2lb loaf tin and a 9-inch springform tin; for brownies, an 8-inch square brownie tin. You can add a muffin tin and a cupcake/bun tin to your repertoire if you like, and these can be used to make mini tarts too. For bigger tarts, stick to loose-bottomed metal tins – 12 inches is a good size. Don't use ceramic dishes for tarts or you'll have a perpetually soggy bottom.

And that's all you need. You could buy a bundt tin or little loose-bottomed tart tins for that occasional professional finish, but you can always adapt every recipe to fit what you've got.

A lined brownie tin or a 7-inch sandwich tin make great tarts, for example. Similarly, line any roasting tray or high-sided pan with a couple of layers of greased tin foil and you've got a way to easily lift out baked goods. This is known as 'tin hacking' – taking something that shouldn't be a tin and making it work.

## YOUR PHONE

Timing is of variable importance in baking, but those who don't want a raw or burnt cake set a timer. I set my alarm for 5-10 minutes before I think it's going to be ready and check it, just in case. And the best timer? Your phone. Keep it in your pocket/bag and it will always be your reminder. Several times I've gone out, only to be reminded 5 minutes into my journey that there's something in the oven. Sometimes I don't get home in time to save the baking, but at least I've saved the house.

Phones are awesome for googling stuff on the fly, too. What can I say? I'm very happy with this book, but sometimes we all forget something.

## USUALLY UNNECESSARY, EXPENSIVE, BUT...
# SOMETIMES DESIRABLE EQUIPMENT

### SIEVE

Does your flour have bugs crawling through it? No? Well get rid of your sieve then. There's no need to sieve flour in cake-making.

You might say that you need it to pass custards and crème pats through, but this is again incorrect. If you need to pass your creation through a sieve to remove lumps, you've done it wrong and you should revisit the guide.

The only things I use a sieve for are dusting icing sugar (to cover up the burnt bits) and straining sauces and puréed fruits whilst cooking. I just like to feel cheffy. You might like to too.

### ELECTRIC MIXER

A handheld electric mixer isn't vital, but it is an excellent investment. It makes mixing relatively effortless, which means you're more likely to do it in the first place. And you can get them for less than a tenner in your local supermarket (keep the receipt though, just in case).

You definitely don't need a stand mixer. All this enables you to do is go and do something else whilst your butter is creaming or your icing is whipping. And most of the time you'll want to keep an eye on whatever you're whipping anyway, or you'll spend half your time with it switched off so you can scrape down the sides of the bowl. I've got a kMix and a KitchenAid and I rarely use them, except for the occasional baking extravaganza.

I do take down a mixer from the top of the fridge for two specific tasks, however: Italian meringue, because it means I can slowly pour my sugar syrup whilst whisking all the time. And genoise sponges, because I'm lazy.

## FOOD PROCESSOR

Some people swear by their food processors when making pastry. I don't, as it makes a worse pastry than you can achieve by hand. A food processor is useful for grinding nuts when you can't find the ground variety, getting lumps out of the ground nuts and icing sugar when making macarons, making marzipan and for chopping onions really fast. And not much else.

## PIPING BAG & NOZZLES

You don't need a piping bag very often, if I'm honest – making things look pretty is the main reason, followed by really round macarons – although I must admit that I'm actually quite a fan of having them around in disposable form. The big, grippy ones from Lakeland are awesome, but you could use a large freezer bag instead. Nozzles are a different story. You can buy packs with hundreds of different nozzles that come in fancy display cases. Don't do it. If you want some pretty nozzles, find a few you like (I'd go for a closed star, open star and petal) and buy a few of each one because they'll inevitably get lost or stood on.

## DIGITAL THERMOMETER

I'll admit that I enjoy the company of my digital thermometer for reassurance. I know that a cake is done if it's past 90°C. I know that my custard is going to set (eventually) if I take it up past 75°C. And most importantly, I know I've got sugar that is at the perfect soft-ball stage for incorporating into meringue at 118°C.

You don't need a thermometer, though, and I've given guides and tricks for how to tell temperatures in the appropriate recipes. But if you do fancy the idea, you can pick one up for about a fiver or so. It will transform your meat cooking, too.

# THE BASICS

# THE BASICS

This chapter takes you step by step through some of the techniques and staples that often seem scary in baking, but are actually nothing to be afraid of. It will focus on reassurance and making things simple, rather than on understanding.

## CRÈME PÂTISSIÈRE

A 'crème pat' is a set custard that can be used as a filling or topping for tarts, cakes, macarons, pastries and pretty much any other bake. It must be sliceable, pipeable, smooth and un-jelly-like. The key is to keep stirring and keep cooking: you don't want the taste of cornflour in the final product, and you don't want it to burn.

Make a chocolate variant by adding a heaped tablespoon of cocoa powder, or a coffee variant by adding a shot of espresso, or a coffee-chocolate variant by adding . . . You get the idea?

*500g whole milk*
*6 egg yolks*
*45g cornflour*
*2 teaspoons vanilla extract (or*
  *seeds from 1 vanilla pod)*

*120g caster sugar*
*50g unsalted butter*

1. Weigh out the milk into a pan, then place on a medium heat. Keep heating until just starting to simmer.

2. In a bowl, whisk together the egg yolks (see page 117 for separating eggs), cornflour, vanilla and caster sugar until completely smooth. You can do this whilst the milk is heating.

3. When the milk is hot, pour half of it onto your eggy mixture and whisk to combine. Then pour this milky-eggy mixture back into the pan with the remaining milk.

4. Keep whisking (or stirring with a wooden spoon, if you prefer) until the crème pat is thick. You're not whisking to incorporate air, but to stop it sticking to the bottom.

5. Once it is as thick as it will go, keep stirring and cooking for another few minutes, just to cook off any starchy flavour. Then remove the pan from the heat and stir for another 30 seconds or so to stop the crème pat sticking to the still-hot pan. Now you can stir in the butter until smooth.

6. Transfer to a jug or bowl and cover with cling film to stop the top drying and a skin forming. Alternatively, you can sprinkle it with icing sugar. Leave to cool, then chill for up to two days.

# THE BEST CRÈME ANGLAISE
## (POURING CUSTARD)

This is the best custard recipe you will ever try, I guarantee. Yes, it's heavy on the egg yolks, but please don't waste the whites: make some meringues, then drown them in said custard. Oh, and I don't hold to this serving custard hot nonsense – cold is best.

1 vanilla pod (or 1 teaspoon
   vanilla paste, or
   2 teaspoons vanilla extract)
250g whole milk

250g single cream
100g caster sugar
6 egg yolks

1. First, slice the vanilla pod in half lengthways and scrape out the seeds using the sharp edge of a knife. Place both seeds and pod into a pan with the milk and cream. Alternatively, use the vanilla paste or extract. Bring to a simmer over a medium heat.

2. While that's heating up, put the caster sugar and egg yolks into a bowl and whisk lightly. When the milky mix is bubbling around the edge, pour half of it onto the eggy mixture and whisk together. Then pour the milky-eggy mixture back into the pan with the remaining milk.

3. Keep whisking all the time, to stop the custard sticking to the bottom of the pan. Reduce the heat to low and cook the custard until it's thickened. It is done when it reaches about 85°C. If you don't have a thermometer, dip a spoon in, remove it, draw a line with your finger on the back of the spoon – if the trail remains, your custard is cooked. Chill and store for up to 3 days.

# CRÈME BRÛLÉE
### MAKES SIX

Not really an ancillary like all the rest in this chapter, but it follows on from custards and it is a useful thing to have up your sleeve if everything else goes awry. Who doesn't like crème brûlée? You can bake it in the oven in a bain marie (ramekins in a tray of water) for about 30–35 minutes, or you can do it this way, which gives a smoother texture. The golden ratio is one large egg yolk to 100ml double cream.

Because we're not baking, I tend to serve it in glass tumblers; they do the trick. Then, for a flourish, add a few berries. You need a blowtorch for the top; a grill causes the top layer of custard to go runny and horrible.

1 punnet of fresh berries
400ml double cream
80g caster sugar,
   plus extra for the top

1 teaspoon vanilla
   paste (or seeds from
   1 vanilla pod, or 2 teaspoons
   vanilla extract)
4 large egg yolks

1. First, prepare six serving glasses or ramekins. Divide the berries between them then place in the fridge to help the custard set quicker.

2. Weigh the cream, sugar, vanilla and egg yolks into a pan. Whisk together and place on a low heat, stirring all the time (I tend to use a balloon whisk).

3. Heat the mixture until it begins to thicken, stirring all the time. Test on the back of a spoon to see if it's done. You want it to hit 85°C (if you have a thermometer).

4. Pour the custard into the prepared glasses and leave to set in the fridge until cold. Just before serving, sprinkle with plenty of caster sugar and blowtorch until brown.

# FRANGIPANE

**Frangipane is basically cake mix made with almonds instead of flour. It is a great tart filling, especially when combined with fruit, cream, custard or crème pat. The quantity below can be added straight into a raw 12-inch pastry case, then topped with glazed fruit for an awesome French tart. You can use any ground nuts, to your own taste, and you can add flour to make it a bit more cake-like.**

*100g softened, unsalted butter*
*100g caster sugar*
*2 medium eggs*
*100g ground almonds*

1. In a bowl, mix the butter and sugar together until paste-like – you don't need to cream as you would for a sponge cake. Make sure the butter is soft before starting; give it a zap in the microwave if necessary.

2. Add the eggs and almonds and mix everything together until it is a pretty even consistency. Unlike flour, you can't really overmix the almonds, but you can turn them from a ground consistency to one a bit more like peanut-butter, so don't go mad with the whisk.

3. This will keep for up to a day in the fridge. To use, simply place it in a pastry case, or inside or on top of puff pastry, then add some fresh fruit and bake.

# CARAMEL
## (& SAVING CRYSTALLISED CARAMEL)

Caramel – hard caramel, for baskets, spun sugar and general baking glue – can be daunting, but learn the rules and it's easy. What you're doing is changing a sugar into an invert sugar – this involves splitting your sugar (sucrose) into its two component sugars (glucose and fructose) through the application of heat. Once there, it's fragile, and any small amount of sucrose or excess stirring (increase in surface area) can lead to a crystallisation chain reaction that causes the whole thing to convert back and thus be ruined . . . But one of the other things that causes sucrose to split apart is acid, so adding the juice of half a lemon and waiting five minutes will save it. As a fail-safe, you can just add lemon juice at the start.

The more humid your environment, the less time the caramel will last. If it's pouring with rain, you're talking minutes for a spun sugar nest. On a hot, dry day, fine cobwebs will last for hours. Do be careful – seemingly cooled caramel can still cause horrific burns.

*100g caster sugar*
*1 dessertspoon water (or juice of ½ lemon)*

1. Into a clean saucepan, weigh the sugar and water. Place it on a medium-high heat to allow the sugar to melt and dissolve in the liquid. At this stage, feel free to stir the sugar gently to help it dissolve, though try not to get any on the sides of the pan – these crystals can lead to disaster (see above).

2. Once the sugar has dissolved, stop stirring. The spoon can start off a crystallisation reaction and ruin your caramel. Bring the syrup to a boil. If using gas, make sure the flames don't lick up the sides of your pan, as this can superheat the sides and start the crystallisation process.

3. Boil the syrup for several minutes, or until it reaches your desired colour – you want a golden brown shade for making baskets and the like. If there's any crystallisation, add a squeeze of lemon juice, remove from the heat for 5 minutes, then boil until it starts to darken again.

4. Once it has reached a nice shade of brown, it's only a few seconds off burning. To stop it going too dark, plunge your pan into a shallow sink of cold water for a few seconds. This should bring it to a perfect working temperature (boiling hot caramel is too liquid).

5. You can experiment with all kinds of shapes: For spun sugar, lightly grease the handle of a wooden spoon. Hold it by the spoon end, and dip a dessertspoon into your liquid caramel. Furiously move this back and forth over the outstretched handle, dipping your spoon back in the caramel as appropriate. As it falls, it will harden into strands. Gather the strands together for a spun sugar nest. For a basket, grease a small bowl with a little vegetable oil. Drizzle your caramel over the bowl in a criss-cross or lattice pattern. The basket, when cooled, should lift out easily. For sugar corkscrews, your caramel needs to be cooled to a 'just workable' temperature: it should only just flow from a spoon. Lightly grease a wooden spoon handle, and twirl it slowly under a stream of caramel (you are moving the wooden spoon, not the pouring spoon).

# EASY CARAMEL SAUCE

This fantastic sauce is referenced again and again through this book. This is a reflection on its simplicity as well as its deliciousness. You don't need a thermometer or any of the usual caramel faff.

*75g unsalted butter*
*100g light brown sugar*
*50g golden syrup*
*125g double cream*
*1 teaspoon flaked sea salt*

1. Weigh your butter, sugar and syrup into a saucepan and place on a medium heat. Stir all the time with a wooden spoon until everything has melted.

2. Bring to the simmer, then remove from the heat and add the double cream and salt. Stir everything to combine. Your sauce is now ready, but watch you don't burn yourself. You can reheat it if it becomes too solid.

# MELTED CHOCOLATE

Tempering chocolate is a massive faff, if I'm honest. But I'll tentatively tell you how to do it, for the results it gives are extremely reliable. You can use it for coating fruit, for all manner of baked goods and their decoration and for making your own chocolate bars.

It's all to do with the 'snapping points' of chocolate. There are six different types of crystal contained within chocolate that melt at different temperatures. Type 1 melts at 17°C, whereas type 6 melts at 36°C. You don't need to know much about types 1, 2, 3 or 4, other than their presence causes that crumbly, gritty texture you get in chocolate if you're involved in reckless melting.

Type 5 is the good stuff, with glossiness, a good snap and a firm texture. This melts at 34°C, so to encourage it to form you need to melt all the crystals by bringing the chocolate to above 36°C. Then you allow it to cool to about 27°C to allow type 4 and 5 crystals to form, then you heat it gradually to about 30°C, melting all your type 4 crystals and leaving just the type 5. Complicated, I know, but if you want to do this you can, using a bowl above a pan of simmering water and a digital thermometer.

Or you can be smart, and take advantage of a simple fact: all the chocolate you buy is already tempered and should only have type 5 crystals in it.

Then you can take advantage of a very simple chemical fact: crystals like being next to other crystals of the same type. So adding unmelted chocolate to melted chocolate encourages the melted chocolate to form crystals of the unmelted chocolate's complexion. Basically, all this means is that rather than tempering chocolate, you can use the following neat trick . . .

1. Break three-quarters of your chocolate into chunks and place in a microwaveable bowl. Using a microwave on low power, slowly melt it for 15 seconds at a time, stirring after each burst to assess progress and to redistribute the heat. You can use a bowl sitting over a pan of gently simmering water if you prefer, but it isn't quite so gentle.

2. Whilst it's melting, chop the final quarter of chocolate as finely as you can.

3. Once the microwaved chocolate has just melted (and I mean *just*), add most of the chopped chocolate and stir. Don't stir vigorously: incorporating too much air can lead to a cloudy finish.

4. Once combined, leave to settle for about a minute. If the incorporated chocolate hasn't amalgamated with the rest, then zap in the microwave for 10-second bursts on low power until melted, then stir in the remaining chunks until melted and combined.

5. This can then be piped (use the microwave again if it hardens too much during piping), drizzled, dipped into or simply dolloped. You may still find any exposed surface is cloudy, though silicone or plastic moulds give an amazing shine, and for a good shine on a flat piece of chocolate, carefully lay some cling film on top.

## CHOCOLATE GANACHE

A chocolate ganache is traditionally a mixture of double cream and chocolate, melted together and then left to set. You can then use a mould, melon baller or just your hands to roll out the paste into chocolate truffles. In recent times, a trend has sprung up for using water instead of double cream in a ganache, cutting out most of the calories and enhancing the chocolate flavour. But it isn't quite as smooth and sumptuous, or as simple to make. You can add butter to both types of ganache for extra richness; I also tend to add a short shot of espresso – you can't taste the coffee, but it brings out the flavour of the chocolate.

*250g double cream (or 100g water)*
*250g dark chocolate*
*a very short shot of espresso (or ½ teaspoon instant coffee granules), optional*
*50g butter, optional*

1. In a saucepan on a low heat, gently heat the cream or water until boiling, stirring regularly to stop it burning.

2. Whilst it's heating, break the chocolate into chunks. If using water, chop the chocolate as finely as you can. Place it in a bowl.

3. Pour the liquid onto the chocolate, adding the coffee and/or butter at the same time. Stir until the chocolate has completely melted.

4. Your ganache should be smooth. If it splits (looks grainy), you can rescue it. Pour half of the ganache into another bowl and place it in the freezer for 10 minutes. Place the other half back in the pan over a low heat. You want to heat it until it all melts again (at least 70°C on a thermometer).

5. Finally, remove the other half from the freezer, pour the hot mixture onto the cold and whisk together with an electric mixer.

6. Your ganache should be stored in the fridge, whether water- or cream-based. Water-based ganaches will set rock hard, however; allow them to come to room temperature before piping or scooping.

# ICING

## BUTTERCREAM

Buttercream is my least favourite icing, not because it is bad, but because it's just so overused – I like the icing part of my cupcakes to be less than the cake component, thanks.

To make a really good buttercream is simple. Take some butter at room temperature and weigh it. Multiply that weight by two, and mix the butter with that quantity of icing sugar. Mix and mix and mix (a lot) until you've got something that's light as a feather and nearly ice-white. This takes a bit of time. You can add all sorts of food colourings, jam, puréed fruit, vanilla, cocoa powder, instant coffee, lemon curd – the recipe stays the same, just add your chosen extras a little at a time, tasting all the time, until you like it. There, that's buttercream dealt with.

## CREAM CHEESE FROSTING

A far superior variant, I believe, is cream cheese frosting. You must use full-fat cream cheese or your icing will never set. This can be made in the same way as buttercream, just with a little more icing sugar – but I believe a more solid example requires a little butter too, and it's a bit more involved, so it's probably worth a recipe.

*50g unsalted butter*
*300g icing sugar*
*125g full-fat cream cheese, chilled*

1. Melt the butter in a bowl in the microwave or in a pan. This is simply to make it easier and faster to incorporate.

2. Once melted, mix the butter into the icing sugar with a wooden spoon. This can be tricky to do without making a powdery mess, so take it easy and don't use an electric mixer unless you've got some kind of shield to stop the sugar flying everywhere.

3. Once you've managed to form a kind of dough, add the cold cream cheese. Now it's time to break out the electric mixer if you have one: whisk everything together for at least 5 minutes; the volume increases slowly and gradually, so give it time. It will become stiffer the more you mix. Your icing is now ready to spread on cakes; it works especially well on carrot cake.

## ITALIAN MERINGUE BUTTERCREAM

I'd have ended this section at the cream cheese frosting if it weren't for one final type of icing that I believe deserves more frequent use than it gets: the Italian meringue buttercream. This is an icing so light, smooth and tasty that even an arch cupcake-hater such as myself won't object to a wee sponge topped with a mountain of this stuff. You have to follow the rules of caramel (see page 27), meringue (see page 220) and buttercream icing (see page 31), so it's a bit tricky. But it's worth it. You'll probably want to use a stand mixer for this, if you have one.

Note: I often thought the reason this icing was so good was the meringue. That's partly the case, but just look at the quantity of butter we're using here . . .

> 225g caster sugar
> 50g cold water
> 3 medium egg whites
> 330g really soft, unsalted butter (soften in the microwave if required)
> a dash of vanilla extract

1. Into a large, clean saucepan, weigh the sugar and water. Place this on a medium-high heat and stir to dissolve the sugar. Once it has turned to liquid, stop stirring and bring to a boil.

2. Whilst it's heating, place the egg whites in a stand mixer and whisk them to stiff peaks.

3. Once your boiling syrup reaches 118°C (or if you don't have a thermometer, when it has been boiling for about 30 seconds), slowly drizzle it into the egg whites, whisking on high speed all the time.

4. Once it is all incorporated, keep whisking for at least 5 minutes to cool the mixture down (it needs to be cool before adding the butter or it will split) and ultimately to make sure your meringue is as consistent as possible.

5. Once cool, reduce to a moderate speed and add the soft butter a wee chunk at a time. You might need to stop and scrape down the sides of the mixer several times. If it doesn't combine, increase the speed and just keep whisking. If it still doesn't combine, chill your bowl in the freezer for 10 minutes then try again.

6. Finally, add a little vanilla extract (or any other flavourings you can think of – see page 23). Chocolate meringue buttercream is especially nice – just whisk in 100g melted dark chocolate after you've incorporated the butter.

# MARZIPAN

Don't like marzipan? Try making your own. That fake cherry flavour doesn't develop for a while, so by making your own you don't need to go through it. Instead, you just get beautiful sweet almondiness. Or maybe you can't stand almonds. That's fine, you can make marzipan with any nut – pistachios work particularly well. If you use blanched nuts, you get a more even colour.

*a pinch of salt*
*1 medium egg white*
*125g blanched or ground almonds (or the nut of your choice)*
*150g icing sugar*

1. In a bowl, add the pinch of salt to the egg white and beat together with a fork.

2. Place the nuts and icing sugar in a food processor. Blend these together until it forms as fine a powder as you can get.

3. Drizzle the egg white slowly into the food processor until a dough is formed.

4. Wrap in cling film and chill for several hours. Because of the sugar, you don't need to worry about the bacteria in the raw egg white, so your marzipan will last as long as shop-bought. The only thing you need to worry about is that almondy flavour.

# CRUMBLE TOPPING

There is no question: this is the best crumble topping. It's life-changing. The filling is up to you – layer up thin slices of fresh fruit with a sprinkling of demerara sugar between each layer and top with this. My favourite is Bramley apple and frozen morello (sour) cherries.

*150g plain flour*
*75g salted butter*
*75g demerara sugar*
*75g rolled oats*

1. Weigh the flour and butter into a large bowl. Rub these together, just as you would for shortcrust pastry (see page 151).

2. Mix in the sugar and oats and continue rubbing until the crumble is of an even consistency.

3. Now squeeze the crumble mixture together, really hard. You want to try to make one big lump.

To use the topping for a fruit crumble, preheat the oven to 180°C/160°C fan/Gas 4. Slice your chosen fruit and use to cover the bottom of a baking dish. Sprinkle with sugar then continue the layers until you've used all the fruit. Break chunks off the crumble lump and scatter these on top of your fruit. You want lumps rather than breadcrumbs for texture. Sprinkle with a little more sugar. Bake for 35–40 minutes and serve hot with custard.

# JAM

Jam is simply reduced fruit mixed with sugar. What causes jams to set is a combination of the sugar – in the same way as caramels or syrups are set – and pectin – a jellifying substance found in many fruits that is not unlike gelatine. Classic jams are made by combining equal quantities of sugar and fruit. Alternatively, you can add less sugar (for example, half sugar to fruit) and reduce for longer to sweeten. You can even make jam that's all fruit, but this doesn't tend to be as nice or last as long. It's the sugar in jam that's the preservative. Just as bacteria can't grow on anything that's got loads of salt in it because the salt dries them out, they can't grow on sugar for the same reason. A microscopic organism may well land on your jam, but once it does, all the water inside will be sucked out, as it flows from areas of low concentration of sugar to high. That's why jam takes ages to go off.

Some jams need added pectin to set – you can buy pectin on its own or mixed into 'jam sugar'. Fruits such as strawberries, blueberries, apricots, figs, peaches and pears need added pectin; others such as raspberries, apples, blackberries, plums, cranberries and citrus fruits contain plenty of pectin.

Finally, if you have a choice between fresh fruit grown in some distant country, or frozen fruit, go frozen every time. Fruit is frozen very soon after picking, and usually in season when yields are highest. It tastes so much better.

*300g of your chosen fruit,*          *150–300g caster sugar*
*fresh or frozen*          *pectin, optional (see above)*

1. Place the fruit and sugar in a pan on a low-medium heat. Try to burst and squish the fruit against the side of the pan as it heats up to make the juice come out, so it doesn't burn.

2. Stir constantly until the sugar has dissolved. Then just let it get on with it. Don't turn up the heat too high or it will burn.

3. Gently simmer until the jam reaches 107°C on a thermometer, or passes the cold plate test: take a wee teaspoon of jam and drop it onto a cold plate. The jam should cool to room temperature quickly. Run a finger through it and if its sides hold, it's done.

4. Remove the jam from the heat and pour into sterilised jars. To sterilise, either run the jars and lids through the dishwasher or carefully rinse with boiling water. Seal with sterilised lids whilst they are still hot. This will pop the safety top back in as they cool down.

# CURD

This wobbly preserve is most often made from lemons, but you can make it with any citrus fruit. Do be warned that if you choose the less sour citrus fruits, the shelf life of your curd won't be quite as long. With lemons or limes, you can make it then store it in sterilised jars for up to two weeks. This recipe is sharp and not overly thick. Try to find unwaxed fruit, or scrub them first.

*200g caster sugar*
*100g unsalted butter, diced*
*4 large lemons, 6–8 limes, 2 small grapefruit or 2 large oranges*
*2 medium eggs, plus 2 egg yolks*

1. First, prepare a bowl that will sit over a pan of simmering water without touching the water. Into the bowl, add the sugar, diced butter and the juice and zest of your chosen fruit, then mix to combine.

2. Heat over the pan of simmering water to melt the butter, then add the eggs and yolks and whisk everything together.

3. Heat for a good 10 minutes or so, stirring all the time with a whisk or wooden spoon. As you stir, it will gradually thicken up – when it's like a thick, gloopy custard, you know it's done.

4. Pour immediately into sterilised jars and keep in the fridge for a couple of weeks. Or place in a jug, cover with cling film and keep for up to a few days in the fridge. Fold into whipped double cream to make an instant syllabub.

# PIPING

## TECHNIQUE

If you're a bit sceptical, don't treat this section with complete disdain. Piping is difficult. Or, more accurately, good piping is difficult and requires a lot of practice. It doesn't require a million different types of nozzle, as some would have you believe; you really just need a freezer bag to get started, though I'd recommend disposable plastic piping bags if you can find them.

## SIMPLE PIPING

1. Roll up the top edges of your piping bag to make the bag smaller and easier to load with icing or cream. You will be holding the piping bag with your hand just underneath this rolled-up top lip.

2. Using a scraper or spatula, scoop your icing into the bag, pressing down to create a flat surface over the opening (think of the icing as Polyfilla). This helps you avoid airpockets by creating one big air pocket we can get rid of later on.

3. Scoop in more icing, always creating a flat surface and thus avoiding the incorporation of any pockets of air that will disrupt your piping stream. The only pocket allowed is the one at the tip.

4. Once filled, unroll the remaining bag and twist it very tightly at the top to squeeze your filling into the tip – you can hold on to this twisty end for steady control.

5. Cut off the tip of the bag to your desired size with sharp scissors – this needs to be done in one clean cut, otherwise you will have a ragged edge and thus ragged piping.

6. Using your dominant hand, hold on to the twisted edge of the piping bag. This is the hand you'll be using to squeeze (always squeeze from the top). For supreme steadiness, place the edge of your non-dominant hand underneath the piping bag, a few centimetres back from the tip.

7. Piping itself requires a bit of a knack and it's very difficult to explain here. If you're piping patterns or lines, you need to co-ordinate your squeezing pressure and your movement; *fluidity* of movement is key. You should almost pipe just above what you're piping onto, rather than directly on top.

8. Piping dollops and peaks is easier – your opening should be smaller than the size you want to pipe. Start with the tip of the bag right down onto your surface and squeeze firmly to cause a ballooning effect. When you're done, press down very quickly with the bag, then lift up just as you stop piping for a nice, even dollop. For a big, tall peak, gently lift the bag whilst tapering off your squeezing pressure.

## PATTERNS

Admittedly, with different nozzles, you can add hundreds of quite beautiful and often tacky effects to your baking. But the fact is, you don't need many; you definitely don't need a magnificent piping set that comes in a big briefcase.

If you want to get into fancy piping, my tip would be to buy a big roll of disposable piping bags and just a few solid metal nozzles: a large 'open' star, a wee 'closed' star and a petal tip will be enough to start you off. All you need to do is snip a hole in your piping bag before filling, shove the nozzle into the end, then fill. Here are a few examples of what you can do with just a large star tip:

1. Simple large stars. Pipe these onto cupcakes and fairy cakes by squeezing hard then lifting off gently.

2. Swirls. As above, but twist the piping bag as you remove it.

3. Straight lines. Use the star tip to create interesting-shaped eclairs, or down the length of cakes for a neat finish.

4. Shells. A classic, used around the edges of cakes to conceal any unsightly or unwanted bits. Simply squeeze as if you were making a star, and as you ease off on the pressure, rotate and pull your bag away horizontally.

5. Mr Whippy. The typical swirl that often adorns cupcakes. Start in the middle, spiralling your way out to the sides then gradually build a cone shape to the top.

# ICING SUGAR

It may seem odd to have a section detailing the awesomeness of icing sugar, but it really can turn ugly piles of (tasty) gunge into beautiful snow-covered peaks, with the right application. You would not believe the sins that I have covered with icing sugar.

Check out the following simple steps to the perfect icing sugar finish. Never ever dust straight from the packet through a sieve and onto a cake, or straight from the pack itself.

1. Locate a fine sieve or tea-strainer, and place it on an easily wiped surface.

2. Gently fill the sieve with icing sugar.

3. To dust, tap the sieve against your other hand above your cake, to cause a light sprinkle of icing sugar to fall. Practise above your surface first to make sure you've got the hang of it.

# WHIPPED CREAM
## (CRÈME CHANTILLY)

Whipping cream is not like whipping meringue; you can take it too far with just a few soft beats – so easily, in fact, that I'd recommend whipping with a hand whisk (unless very large volumes are involved). Whipping is possible thanks to the fat in the cream; you unfurl the fat globules, allowing them to form an emulsion with the air. Fat is essential, therefore, so you need cream that's relatively fatty (double cream) for a stable whipped product. You can whip single cream, but it won't stay whipped for long and it won't taste as yummy.

1. Before you start, chill your bowl in the freezer and make sure the cream is chilled in the fridge. This will help the fat stay in solution and give you a more solid mixture. Think how unyielding chilled butter is compared to soft butter; it's the same fats we're working with.

2. Pour the cream into the chilled bowl – it's best to use more than you think you need. Then add a dash of vanilla paste or extract and a few tablespoons of caster sugar. These are both purely for flavour, though the sugar may have a role in stabilising the mixture.

3. Whip the cream using a hand whisk. You want to incorporate air, and there's no specific technique for doing this; anything that causes splashing is fine. You want to keep whipping until you feel a little resistance.

4. Once you feel some resistance, the cream is very nearly done (though it may not look it). At this point, focus on getting all the cream to the same consistency by mixing in the more liquid parts with the more formed parts. Your cream should now be glossy and just about hold its shape.

5. Give it a couple more whips just to bring it to a 'stiff' stage – if you notice any graininess, STOP. Your cream can now be stored ready to serve.

6. If you do take it too far and your cream curdles, don't despair. Whack an electric mixer on full blast and keep whisking until you have a completely separated mixture. Take the solid yellow stuff, compress it in a piece of muslin or a tea towel and admire your own homemade butter.

# FILO PASTRY

The reason I don't have a chapter on how to make filo pastry is that I don't believe you should make it at home. It's the kind of thing you might want to make once, just to see how much faff it is, then never consider again. It's much more efficient for it to be produced on a commercial scale. If you're absolutely insistent, the internet will help.

You can do anything you like with shop-bought filo, and you can use it in any situation where puff, shortcrust or sweetcrust would be appropriate. Use at least four layers to make sure your bakes have enough support. And for flavour and puff, you want plenty of melted butter brushed between the sheets. For more of a crackly effect, you can sprinkle sugar between the layers too.

The two things I'm always asked about are baklava and strudel. I don't think they require a strict recipe once you know how to make them; I always use measurements such as 'handfuls'.

## BAKLAVA

Layer square sheets of filo in a roasting tray, brushing a good drench of melted butter in between each. Every four or five layers or so, sprinkle with a load of chopped nuts, some sugar, and spices of your choice, topping with more filo, and then bake at 180°C/160°C fan/Gas 4 until crisp. You should aim for at least 4 layers of nuts.

Once that's done, drizzle with sugar syrup made with equal quantities of sugar and water and a touch of orange blossom water to flavour. It's that easy.

## STRUDEL

Mix six peeled, cored and chopped apples in a bowl with a handful of raisins, a teaspoon of mixed spice and a few tablespoons of brown sugar. Layer your filo on a lined baking tray, brushing plenty of melted butter between each layer. After 6–8 layers, sprinkle over a couple of tablespoons of dried couscous or breadcrumbs, to absorb the water released during baking. Then add your apple mixture along the length of the filo and roll up, folding over at the ends and placing the seam on the bottom. Brush the top with more butter and bake for 40 minutes or so at 180°C/160°C fan/Gas 4.

You can use any fruit, either stewing it first to dry it out, or adding couscous or breadcrumbs as described, to absorb the excess water.

OPPOSITE: GRANNY'S SPONGE

# CAKE

# CAKE

I'm treading with care in this chapter, as there are many who have very strong opinions on cake (and cake decorating) who may disagree with me.

'Cake' can describe many similar but distinct objects. The first is a finished centrepiece made up of single or multiple baked layers that is then assembled or decorated using sugar, jam, icings, cream, fruit and other confectionery. It can be small or large and any shape you like. But this isn't what I'm focusing on here. I'm going to go through the important bits – the substance that opposes the style that has engulfed cake-making to the point of profound irritation. By the time most intricately decorated cakes are complete, you might as well have iced the tin. A cake is for eating, not looking at.

My definition of 'cake' is a sponge-like base made with eggs, sugar, butter (or margarine) and flour of roughly equal quantities, with a pinch of raising agent. The traditional 'creaming' method involves beating butter and sugar together to create bubbles. Then eggs are added gradually to multiply and expand those bubbles, and flour is 'folded' in with gentle strokes so as not to develop its gluten. The 'all in one method' is the quicker, easier and riskier method that involves using margarine as opposed to butter. All the ingredients are simply whisked together until light, but this invariably results in a more resiliently textured, bread-like sponge.

## THE IDEAL CAKE

The ideal cake should be an even, pale golden brown colour on all sides. The top should not be overly domed or dipped; it should be flat to mildly domed. The cake should not peak towards its edges, and there should be no hard or snappy crust; any brown areas should be soft and springy.

The texture should be mildly resilient (bouncy), but should tear or cut with ease. It should not be distinctly wet nor should it be bread-like or overly aerated. When cut with a straight, sharp knife, it should shed moist crumbs; it should not need a bread knife. The inside should be a pale to deep golden colour, depending on the happiness of the hens who provided the eggs.

The taste should be a good balance between indulgent and light. There should be a prominent buttery flavour and some richness provided by the egg yolks, but no detectable taste of raising agent. It should be easy to eat, and should not be cloying, stodgy or dry.

## BASIC CAKE RECIPE
### MAKES ONE 8-INCH SANDWICH CAKE OR ONE DEEP SINGLE-LAYER 9-INCH CAKE

*250g softened, salted butter*
*250g caster sugar*
*5 medium eggs (approximately 250g), at room temperature*
*250g self-raising flour*
*1 teaspoon baking powder*
*a little milk, to loosen*

### TIN

Line the bottom of two loose-bottomed cake tins with baking paper, either by stretching the paper over the loose bottom or by cutting out precise circles and placing these on the bottom. Then grease the whole tin with butter or margarine, especially the corners. Finally, sprinkle in a little flour and bash it around to coat the greased surface. Discard any excess, or transfer it to another tin.

### CREAM

Weigh the soft butter and sugar into a large bowl. Smoosh the butter into the sugar to combine, then beat it (hard) with a wooden spoon or an electric mixer until smooth. Keep beating until it has changed to a lighter colour (almost white) and is of noticeably greater volume.

### EGGS

Break the eggs into a separate bowl first (even expert egg-breakers get shell in the mix), then add them, one at a time, into the large bowl. You should beat well after each addition. It does not matter if the mix curdles.

### WHY

Sticking to the tin is one of the most frequent cake disasters and is easily averted. The bottom of the tin should always be lined; a knife can be inserted down the sides of any tin to free them, but this is more difficult with the bottom. The fat in the butter then lubricates the tin to stop sticking, and the flour prevents the surface of the cake becoming greasy and provides an extra barrier.

### WHY

By 'creaming' the butter and sugar together, we're creating lots of tiny air bubbles within the mix, so that we end up with something that looks not dissimilar to whipped cream. This is done by tearing wee holes in the butter with the sharp edges of the sugar. The large fatty (non-polar) molecules of the butter then repel each other so that the bubbles remain. This is an emulsion between butter and air.

### WHY

Now we are creating a liquid emulsion (mixture of fat and liquid), just like when making a mayonnaise. This is why it is important to add the eggs gradually – adding them all at once will cause it to split into a half eggy, half buttery mix that will give an inconsistent texture. It is important to beat at a high speed to turn the modest number and size of bubbles created in the creaming stage into large, stable ones. Curdling has been shown not to affect the final rise.

### FOLD

Add the flour and baking powder on top, gently combining the baking powder into the flour with your fingertips. There's no need to sieve. 'Fold' everything together gently with a metal spoon until there is no flour visible: scoop from the bottom and sides of the bowl and dump the spoon's contents on top. Turn the bowl a little and repeat. Work the mix as little as possible. Do not use an electric mixer.

### WHY

It's best to mix the baking powder into your flour first for even distribution and an even texture. 'Folding' is gentle and minimal for two reasons: you don't want to force out the air you've already whipped into the mixture, and (more importantly) you don't want to develop too much gluten in the flour. Try to use a metal spoon for simple mechanical reasons: the sharp, thin sides allow you to cut down to the bottom of the bowl with minimum disruption to the mix.

### WOBBLE

After the folding, your mix may be perfect. It should be of a 'dropping' consistency, gently flopping from the spoon when it is tilted. When shaken, it should at least wobble. If your mix is too dry, add a splash of milk and then gently mix it in with your spoon.

### WHY

A mix with too many dry ingredients will be crumbly, and rise with a large dome in the middle; equally, a mix with too much milk or egg will sink in the middle and the texture will be too wet. The dropping consistency is a good compromise and a guide as to when you've got it right. The variation is caused by egg size.

### FILL

Scoop your mix into the prepared tins, placing alternate scoops in each to divide it equally between them. If you've got electric scales, use these to check they are even. Smooth the tops with a spatula or scraper and shake the tins from side to side.

### WHY

Try to make sure the tins are filled as evenly as possible, otherwise, the heat will penetrate through the smaller cake faster, causing it to cook faster. When both cakes are finally cooked, the smaller one will be drier than it should be.

## THE BAKE

Baking a cake depends greatly on the size of the cake and the finish wanted. The standard temperature to bear in mind is 180°C/160°C fan/Gas 4 – this is quoted in the vast majority of recipes out there. However, if your tin is particularly full and deep, or you're baking in a loaf tin, for example, do drop this as low as 160°C/140°C fan/Gas 3. This will stop the outside of the cake burning before the inside has cooked. Equally, if you're making wee fairy cakes or similar, feel free to go up to 200°C/180°C fan/Gas 6.

Timing is all about the thickness of the sponge; how easy it is for the heat to penetrate to the middle. For a standard sponge, you'll want to check it after around 20 minutes. If the top springs right back when pressed, it is done. If not, give it 5 more minutes. For a deep loaf tin or a large mix, it can take much longer – check after 40 minutes. With larger, deeper mixes, you can't rely on its springiness, so insert a skewer or thin knife and if it is clean when removed, it is done. If you have a thermometer, it should be anything over 90°C in the middle. A shallower cake or fairy cakes can be done in 10–15 minutes, so please check them early on.

It is important not to let the oven cool during the early stages of baking, lest the fragile, aerated mix cool down and thus shrink and collapse, leaving you with a sunken cake. Therefore, do not open the oven door during the early stages unless absolutely necessary. It's fine to do so quickly, say, to shove another cake tin in, but don't leave it open for any length of time.

After baking, there's no real need to cool the cake on a cooling rack. Cool in the tin for at least 15 minutes, but don't leave it for hours or it will weld itself to the sides.

## VARIATIONS

COCOA  To make a chocolate cake, add 2–4 heaped tablespoons of cocoa powder to the recipe on pages 42–44 (with the flour and baking powder), depending on how rich you like it. You will need to increase the quantity of milk added.

DRIED FRUIT  A fruit cake is the Victoria sponge mix on page 42 with a load of dried fruit added after the flour. It's that simple. I'd add a couple of teaspoons of mixed spice too, and possibly a tablespoon of treacle. The key is the fruit – add any sort you like, but add a mixture. The total weight of fruit should be *exactly twice* the weight of your flour. Bake low and slow.

BERRIES  If making a loaf or deep cake, add a wee punnet of berries to your flour before you fold it in and toss everything around. This will stop them sinking and breaking apart. If making a cake less than 5cm deep, scatter the berries on top (they'll sink a bit during baking).

CARROTS AND OTHER VEGETABLES  To the basic recipe, add 250g of your chosen (coarsely grated) vegetable and a handful each of chopped nuts and dried fruit. Fold them in after the flour and then loosen as required. Carrots, parsnips, celeriac, courgette, beetroot and aubergine all work well, adding lingering moistness with some subtle flavour.

NUTS  Adding whole or roughly chopped nuts is easy; just fold them in with the flour. A couple of handfuls will do. Adding ground nuts is a bit more difficult as they can dry the cake out. For every 100g of ground nuts, reduce the flour by 50g.

**DRIZZLE**  Making a lemon, lime, orange or grapefruit drizzle cake is simple. Cream the grated zest of the fruit with the butter and sugar, increase the flour in the basic recipe by 25g and don't add any extra milk. Make a syrup by heating the juice of the fruit with 100g caster sugar, then pour on to the cooked (but not cooled) cake. You can pierce the cake to help the syrup infusion.

**BANANA**  A beautiful, moist banana cake or bread can be made by adding one small banana for every 50g of flour. Then halve the quantities of butter and eggs. Positively healthy.

## SUBSTITUTIONS

**'ALL IN ONE'**  Always bear in mind, if you're pushed for time, that there's no shame in using the 'all in one' method and replacing the butter with baking margarine (Stork). Simply mix all the ingredients together until light (about 30 seconds). Do remember that butter is both tastier and healthier (baking margarine is full of bad trans fats), but this works well with drizzle cakes.

**FLOUR AND RAISING AGENT**  These can easily be replaced, gram for gram, with gluten-free alternatives. Many millers and farms now produce a pre-mixed gluten-free plain flour substitute that works very well. Equally, you can replace the flour (again, gram for gram) with ground almonds, then add half that quantity again of polenta for a beautiful, crumbly cake.

**EGGS**  Of course, eggs can be replaced with recognised vegan egg substitutes, or if you just haven't got quite enough eggs for the size of sponge you'd like, use as many as you can then mix in 50g of milk, yoghurt, buttermilk or sour cream for every egg missed. You want your mix a little on the dry side, however, as these don't have the reinforcing properties of egg.

**SUGAR**  Sugar can be replaced with equal quantities of xylitol, though not normal sweeteners, as the latter produce a dense texture and a strange, astringent taste. These new sweeteners can give you an upset stomach and contain only minimally fewer calories than sugar. You can replace caster with granulated or brown, but cream the mixture for longer.

## STORAGE

The storage of cakes is affected by the amount of fat in them – higher fat cakes stay moist for longer. Regardless, I advocate the storage of undecorated cakes wrapped in cling film and placed back into their original cake tins, if possible. This stops them getting bashed. These keep for a maximum of about three or four days at room temperature. Cakes with a drizzle or syrup keep moist particularly well. If you want to store your cake for longer, freezing is a brilliant way to store it. Wrap your cooled cake as above, then place in the freezer for up to a year.

When storing decorated cakes, consider which ingredient is likely to spoil first, and only then give the cake an appropriate shelf life. For example, if a cake contains fresh cream, you should keep it chilled (until an hour or so before serving) and enjoy within a day. This is the only acceptable time a cake should be in the fridge.

# TROUBLESHOOTING

*Why has my cake sunk in the middle*? This happens when the fragile matrix of the cake can't support its own weight. The most common reasons are an oven temperature that's too low, opening the oven door during early baking, and (less likely) beating too much air in at the start.

*Why does my cake have a big dome or cracks on top*? Three main possible causes: the first is a high oven temperature; a lower temperature gives a flatter rise. The second is a mix that's too dry and needs slackening a little with some milk. The final possibility is a mix that's been overworked so that too much gluten has developed.

*Why is my cake burned on the outside and raw in the middle*? Your oven temperature is too high. Try turning it down by 20°C and letting the heat slowly penetrate into the middle.

*Why is my cake taking ages to cook?* Two main possibilities: a really big cake, or an oven that's a bit off. Invest in an oven thermometer or try upping the temperature. Another option could be too much liquid in your mix, so that the bake is naturally going to be soggy.

*Why is my cake bready/has big bubbles?* This is generally caused by overmixing, especially when using the 'all in one' method. Always remember the gentle folding of the flour at the end; every movement develops the gluten.

*Why didn't my cake rise?* The two main possibilities here are insufficient beating (both during the creaming and the incorporation of the eggs) and insufficient raising agent. The latter can be due to forgetting it altogether, not adding enough, or, more commonly than you might think, out-of-date baking powder. It doesn't have a long shelf life. The same applies to self-raising flour.

*Why has my cake exploded everywhere?* Well done, you've beaten too much air into your mix. The most common occurrence here is if you used the creaming method with fats or margarines designed for making an all in one cake. Alternatively, your cake tins may be too small. I always like to have at least the same space again after smoothing out the mixture.

*Why is my cake soggy?* It is possible that your cake is still raw; make sure it's properly springy before taking it out. You could try adding less liquid next time (check the size of your eggs).

*Why is my cake squint*? If you've got a fan oven, this will blow your cake wonky, so move the cake away from the fan. Otherwise, it's probably due to either inadequate smoothing of the cake before it goes in the oven or putting your tins in a wee bit askew. If you're always getting squint cakes, get a spirit level and check your cooker and oven shelves are perfectly flat.

*Why is my cake dry?* This is due to overbaking, for the most part. The cake should be taken out as soon as it turns springy; even 5 extra minutes could dry it out. Another reason is not enough liquid – remember to add milk until the mixture reaches a 'dropping' consistency.

# GRANNY'S SPONGE

MAKES ONE 7-INCH VICTORIA SPONGE

No cream. No icing. No chocolate. No fruit.

This is a Victoria sponge (incidentally, not a sponge, see the next chapter) at its purest and thus its best. Yes, I occasionally enjoy the odd one filled with whipped cream, lashings of fresh strawberries and maybe a pretty flower on top, but Gran would be distraught.

This is the second recipe I ever baked in my life, and certainly one of the first committed to memory. Some may say the stout 7-inch cake tin should only be used as a Frisbee, but I feel it is the perfect, unobtrusive and quietly reserved size for this cake. Charmingly aloof, even. And it means you aren't at risk of a stroke if you scoff the whole thing in a sitting. Whenever I'm back in Shetland, I still use Gran's old cake tins with a blade that sits on the bottom so that when you swivel it round it unsticks the cake. Glorious.

*75g softened, salted butter*
*75g soft baking margarine*
*150g caster sugar*
*3 medium eggs (approximately*
*    150g without shells), at*
*    room temperature*

*150g self-raising flour*
*½ teaspoon baking powder*
*a little milk, to loosen*
*jam, for the middle*
*a dusting of caster sugar,*
*    for the top*

1. Preheat your oven to 190°C/170°C fan/Gas 5. Draw around the bottom of two 7-inch cake tins onto some baking paper. Cut out these circles and stuff them into the tins, using some butter to make them stick. Finally, grease your tins well and dust with a touch of flour.

2. Into a large bowl, weigh the soft butter, margarine and caster sugar. Using a wooden spoon or an electric whisk, beat these together for several minutes until smooth, pale, creamy and light. This will take at least 5 minutes; you can wrap a tea towel around the bottom of your bowl to secure it.

3. Add the eggs, one at a time, beating well after each addition. It doesn't matter if the mix curdles.

4. Fold in the (unsieved) flour and baking powder with a large metal spoon until the mix is still a wee bit lumpy but no flour is visible. If it's not of the consistency where it will drop easily from a shaken spoon, stir in a tablespoon or two of milk.

5. Divide the mix equally between your two cake tins and bake for 15–20 minutes, or until the cakes are springy, coming away from the sides and a pale golden brown colour. Once baked, cool in the tins for at least 10 minutes, then transfer to a cooling rack if you wish.

6. One cake should be upside down and one should be the same way up as it was baked. Onto the former, spread a generous amount of your favourite jam, then place the second cake on top to make a sandwich. Sprinkle some caster sugar over the top to finish. Ideally, enjoy within a day, but it will keep for several.

# PEAR & VANILLA UPSIDE-DOWN CAKE

MAKES ONE SINGLE-LAYER 9-INCH CAKE

Pear and vanilla is a flavour combination that bridges the gap between traditional and modern, classical and contemporary. But it has gone through a renaissance recently, since some boffins detected the same aroma compounds in both ingredients using a computer.

Except you didn't need a computer to tell you that. Take a good sniff of both; it doesn't take a lot of expensive equipment to work out the similarities.

I tried this combo with parsnips on my first day on *The Great British Bake Off*, and although there was parsnip flavour there, it didn't come through as much as I'd hoped. You can try it if you like: add 250g of grated parsnips after the flour and bake for a bit longer.

| | |
|---|---|
| 250g softened, salted butter | **For the top (or is it bottom?)** |
| 250g caster sugar | 4 pears, preferably Williams |
| 4 medium eggs | or Conference, peeled and |
| 75g Greek-style yoghurt | thinly sliced |
| seeds from 1 vanilla pod | 100g salted butter |
| 260g self-raising flour | 200g caster sugar |
| 1 teaspoon baking powder | juice of ½ lemon |

1. First, line the bottom of a 9-inch springform tin with baking paper, and then grease it well. Preheat your oven to 170°C/150°C fan/Gas 3, and place a tray or piece of foil on the bottom to catch any caramel drips.

2. Prepare the upside-down bit. Make the caramel by heating your butter, caster sugar and lemon juice together in a pan, stirring all the time until melted. Pour this onto the base of your tin and arrange the pears on top.

3. Into a large bowl, weigh the butter and sugar. Using an electric whisk or a wooden spoon, beat them together until smooth, light and creamy – this will take at least 5 minutes.

4. Add the eggs, one at a time, beating well after each addition. Then add the yoghurt and scrape in the vanilla seeds and beat them in as you did the eggs. Smooth would be nice, but this is likely to curdle and don't worry if it does.

5. Gently fold in the flour and baking powder using a large metal spoon, just enough to combine. If it isn't at a dropping consistency, stir in a touch more yoghurt.

6. Carefully pour your mix onto your fruit and bake in the oven for approximately 40–50 minutes, or until golden brown and springy and a skewer comes out clean.

7. Leave to cool for at least 15 minutes before removing the sides of the tin (running a knife around the edge if necessary) then placing a plate or cake stand on top of it. Turn the whole thing upside down before carefully peeling away the base paper. Serve hot or cold.

# BANANA FAIRY CAKES WITH PECAN ICING

MAKES 12 WEE FAIRY CAKES OR 6 BIG CUPCAKES/MUFFINS

Cakes with fruit as a fabric of their assembly sometimes work and sometimes don't. Evidently, it depends on the fruit and how much of it there is. Bananas lend themselves to this cause particularly well – they add tons of softness and moisture, so you've got to cut back on the bits that provide these in the first place: the butter and the eggs. The blubbery bits, conveniently.

You can make these as larger cupcakes, but I hate cupcakes, those overfrosted American deities of evil. We must be nearing the end of this fad now, mustn't we?

With fairy cakes, cook them at a high temperature for a quick bake and so they dome up beautifully in the oven. If you don't like the idea of doing all the fancy caramel stuff, just make the icing without the praline, cut the dome off, cut it in half, and use the icing to make them into banana butterfly cakes.

125g caster sugar
65g softened, salted butter
½ teaspoon vanilla extract
2 bananas (the blacker
    the better)
1 medium egg
125g plain flour
1½ teaspoons baking powder

For the praline:
100g pecan halves
200g caster sugar
juice of 1 lemon

For the pecan icing:
250g icing sugar
100g full-fat cream cheese
sea salt, optional

1. Preheat your oven to 200°C/180°C fan/Gas 6. Line a bun tin with fairy cake cases, or grease the holes of a muffin tin with plenty of butter.

2. Into a large bowl, weigh out the sugar, butter, vanilla, bananas and egg. Using a wooden spoon, beat them all together until the bananas are smashed into the mix.

3. Very carefully, fold in the flour and baking powder until just incorporated. Divvy up the mix into your fairy cake tins; about a heaped teaspoon in each. If you find any bits of flour during the dividing, gently stir them in.

4. Bake your cakes for 10–15 minutes, or until golden brown and very springy to the touch. Leave them to cool in the tin. (At this point, if your pecan halves are unroasted, you can chuck them into the oven on a baking tray at the bottom for 10 minutes too.)

5. While the cakes cool, you can make the praline, though if you're planning on storing, always prepare caramels on the day of eating. Tear off a large piece of baking paper and scatter your pecan halves over half of it; a sprinkle of sea salt wouldn't go amiss here, either. In a pan, heat the caster sugar and lemon juice together over a high heat, stirring all the time until the sugar

has dissolved. Continue to heat over a medium heat until it has turned a golden brown colour. If you need to stir it, swirl the pan. (See my guide to caramel on page 27.) Pour your golden caramel onto your pecans.

6. Once the pecan praline is hard (shouldn't take long), put half of it in a blender or food processor and blitz to a powder. Add the icing sugar and cream cheese and continue blending until smooth. Smash the other half of the praline with a rolling pin for arranging on top.

7. Dollop (or pipe, if you insist) some icing on top of your cakes, then place your caramel decorations and the smashed praline on top in any way you wish.

# CELERIAC CAKE WITH STRAWBERRIES & CREAM
MAKES ONE 7- OR 8-INCH SANDWICH CAKE OR ONE SINGLE-LAYER 9-INCH CAKE

'You can't taste the carrots!' Most vegetable-cake virgins are convinced to take the delicious plunge when a friend explains the veg is there simply for moisture and not flavour. True in the case of carrot cake or courgette cake, but if I wanted only moisture, I'd use the blandest veg I could find for the cake. I want the wondrous subtleties of celeriac to come through here.

I hope celeriac is the next big cake thing; it's awesome. I don't even like the flavour of celery all that much, but I love this. I believe you've got to treat the vegetable with respect, even in a cake. Although it's got a strong celery aroma, it's one that's really quite delicate and works well balanced with fresh fruit flavours, especially strawberry.

And strawberry works exceptionally with black pepper, which doubly brings out the savoury celery tang. And the small amount of lemon zest provides a citrus note that carries the whole cake off lightly.

If you really want to impress someone, blow their mind? Make this cake. It's easy.

200g softened, salted butter
200g caster sugar
grated zest of ½ lemon
½ teaspoon finely ground
   black pepper
4 medium eggs
½ teaspoon vanilla extract
180g plain flour
3 teaspoons baking powder

1 small celeriac, peeled and
   grated (you want about
   200g)
300ml tub of double cream
2–3 tablespoons strawberry jam
1 punnet of fresh strawberries,
   sliced thinly
icing sugar, for dusting

1. Preheat your oven to 180°C/160°C fan/Gas 4. Line the bottom of your tin(s) with baking paper and grease the rest well. Finally, dust with a little flour, bashing away the excess.

2. Into a large bowl, weigh the butter, sugar, zest and pepper. Beat them together with an electric whisk or wooden spoon for at least 5 minutes, until creamy and pale.

3. Add the eggs, one at a time, beating well after each addition. Beat in the vanilla at the same time. If the mix curdles, don't worry.

4. Gently fold in the flour and baking powder until the mix is lumpy but no flour is visible; this should be done in no more than a few large scoops. Finally, dump in the celeriac and fold this in, working the mix as little as possible.

5. Once combined, scoop the mix into your cake tin(s) and bake for 30–40 minutes, depending on the depth. It should be springy and a skewer should come out clean. Leave it to cool in its tin.

6. Once the cake(s) are cool, whip the cream according to the instructions on pages 38–39; don't overwhip. Spread the jam over the cake, top this with about two-thirds of the strawberries and top this with cream. If you're sandwiching, place the other cake on top. Arrange the rest of the strawberries on top in any pretty fashion you like; I'm a fan of the domino effect, plus or minus a liberal dusting of icing sugar. Eat ASAP.

# INSTANT LEMON DRIZZLE

MAKES ONE SINGLE-LAYER 8-INCH CAKE

An emergency cake. It could be because you've got friends coming for dinner and nothing sweet to offer them. It could be because you've promised to bake something for a charity event that's in an hour and a half. It could be as a result of unfathomable, nay, intimate urges. Sometimes we just need cake.

The concept of this cake was taught to me whilst filming for *The Great British Bake Off*. Not by Mary Berry or any of the contestants or crew; this cake comes from the lovely Linda, who owns and runs the country house in the grounds of which *Bake Off* was filmed. She bakes one most mornings for the guests at her B&B and it takes little more than five minutes of her time.

It's a simple, 'all in one' method cake made in a single, wide layer and drizzled with a tart lemon syrup. She adds no zest to the batter, but you can if you like; I tend to as I don't think it takes much extra time and adds a wonderful fresh aroma to the whole thing. The single layer is simple and quick – one tin to line and grease – and the wider and thinner the better; it will cook quicker and the syrup will soak in easier.

*200g baking margarine*
*grated zest of 1 lemon, optional*
*200g caster sugar*
*4 medium eggs*
*200g self-raising flour*

*For the syrup*
*juice of 1 lemon*
*100g caster sugar*

1. Preheat your oven to 180°C/160°C fan/Gas 4. Stuff a torn-off piece of baking paper into an 8-inch springform cake tin (or your tin of choice) – if it covers the sides then there's no need to grease.

2. In a large bowl, whisk together all the cake ingredients with an electric whisk for 20–30 seconds, or until completely combined and slightly pale. Don't overmix.

3. Transfer the mix to your lined cake tin and bake for 25–35 minutes. A skewer should come out clean. For a smaller and deeper cake, go a wee bit longer.

4. When it's nearly done, make the syrup by bringing the lemon and sugar just to a boil in a pan on the hob; drizzle this hot syrup onto your cake as soon as it's out of the oven (reheat if you've underestimated the time the cake has left); you can prick the cake to help the syrup drizzle in if you like.

5. This cake is best enjoyed cool, but is good hot, too – it's more like a pudding, and tastes phenomenal.

# THE BEST CHOCOLATE CAKE

MAKES ONE 8-INCH SANDWICH CAKE

I couldn't get through this chapter without including a chocolate cake, could I?

Here, I want to show you how far you can go: the amplification of flavour that results from the aggregation of marginal changes. Sure, on one end of the spectrum you can whisk a tablespoon or two of cocoa into my standard Victoria sponge recipe. Or you can, from the ground up, taking the structural and flavour characteristics of dark chocolate into account, create a customised chocolate cake recipe.

I'm not saying this is ideal, I'm saying this recipe is what I want from a chocolate cake. Which isn't what I want from a brownie or a chocolate torte, for example. The former I want like a slab of peat, the latter like crumbly compacted compost. This is different. A cake is altogether more formal. A cake should be an occasion. Then we add everything that has been shown to make chocolate better.

Although this cake has a raspberry element, it is there for sharpness rather than flavour. Similarly with the coffee – it brings out the chocolate flavour. The chilli powder imbues the cake with a mere tingle, almost like the warmth of alcohol. The yoghurt cuts through the bitterness of the cocoa. This is a chocolate cake.

Due to the whipped cream, it doesn't keep brilliantly at room temperature, but it doesn't take long to build from its component parts, so do steps 1 to 7 in advance and leave step 8 until just before serving.

*250g softened, salted butter*
*250g caster sugar*
*a wee extra pinch of table salt*
*100g good dark chocolate*
*4 medium eggs*
*a short shot of espresso*
*(or 2 teaspoons instant*
*coffee granules dissolved in hot water)*
*½ teaspoon hot chilli powder,*
*optional*
*1 teaspoon chocolate extract,*
*optional*
*200g natural yoghurt*
*100g high-quality cocoa powder*
*250g plain flour*
*3 teaspoons baking powder*

*For the whipped cream*
*150ml double cream*
*a dash of sugar and vanilla*
*seeds or extract*

*For the raspberry ganache*
*130g fresh raspberries*
*200g dark chocolate*
*pinch of salt*

*For the mirror glaze*
*2 leaves (4g) gelatine*
*100ml double cream*
*100g caster sugar*
*50g cocoa powder*

1. Preheat your oven to 180°C/160°C fan/Gas 4. Draw around two 8-inch sandwich tins onto baking paper and use these discs to line the bottom of each tin. Grease the sides well.

2. In a large bowl, beat the butter, sugar and salt together with an electric whisk or wooden spoon until light, fluffy and almost white in colour – this will take at least 5 minutes. Whilst you're doing this, you can melt the chocolate slowly in the microwave or over a pan of hot water on the hob.

3. Add the eggs to the creamed butter and sugar, one at a time, whisking well after each addition. Then gradually whisk in all the melted chocolate. At this point, add the coffee, chilli (if using), chocolate extract (if using) and yoghurt and whisk them in too. Don't worry if the mixture curdles.

4. Finally, dump the cocoa, flour and baking powder on top (using your fingers to disperse the baking powder into the flour) and fold them in as gently as you can. Pour the mix into your cake tins and bake for 30–40 minutes on the middle shelf, or until springy and a skewer comes out clean.

5. Leave in the tins to cool whilst you make the fillings. For the whipped cream, whisk the cold cream, sugar and vanilla in a cold bowl until just coagulated (see my guide on pages 38–39). Cover and set aside.

6. For the raspberry ganache, first blitz the raspberries in a blender then pass them through a sieve to remove any bits. Place this purée in a pan with the salt and bring to the boil. Whilst it's heating, chop the chocolate into small pieces and place in a bowl. As soon as the raspberry purée is boiling, add in your chocolate and mix together until smooth. Cover and leave to cool to room temperature. (If you have any trouble, see my section on ganache on pages 30–31.)

7. For the mirror glaze, soak the two leaves of gelatine in cold water. Place your cream, sugar and cocoa in a pan and heat until just about boiling, stirring all the time. Once hot, strain through a sieve into a jug, then stir in the soaked gelatine. Set aside until needed.

8. Steps 1–7 can be done in advance, but build the cake just before serving. Place one cake (the less perfect one) upside down on a plate or cake stand. Spread with a thick layer of the raspberry ganache, making sure you can see it at the sides. Then top this with the whipped cream, again making sure it nearly reaches the sides. Finally, top gently with the other cake. Reheat your mirror glaze in a pan or in the microwave to melt it, then drizzle it over your cake so it drips down the sides.

# SPONGE

# SPONGE

The genoise sponge is an exceedingly light, eternally ingestible sponge. To many, a true sponge should be fatless, but this doesn't have to be the case. The genoise is used to underpin much of French patisserie, though it gets its name from the Italian city of Genoa. A genoise has no need for any additional raising agent, a fact that increases my affection for it – it is pure, without chemical adulteration.

The sponge is made by whisking eggs with sugar and then carefully folding in flour and melted, browned butter ('beurre noisette'). It is these processes that give this amazing sponge its tricky reputation: in the days before electric mixers, it took a prohibitively long time to make well, and many gave up without whipping in sufficient air. Now, with KitchenAids and kMixes galore, eggs swell universally. But then so many people go on to ruin their cake by using the same mixer to incorporate the flour.

The first step requires brute force; the second requires delicate control. Whisk using the mixer then always fold by hand. Combine the two and you've got a beautiful sponge that's so much lighter than your average cake and with great consistency in every sense of the word.

## THE IDEAL SPONGE

The sponge can be any shape and of any depth, though it should not be so deep as to concertina (squish at the bottom) under its own weight or have concave or angled sides. It should be a pale golden brown colour, and should be entirely flat on top if possible – no dome or sinking in the middle.

It should slice easily without significant crumbling. The colour of the crumb should be a very pale lemon to pale gold, depending on the quality of the eggs used. The texture should be exceedingly light and fluffy, and the bubbles should all be of roughly even, regular size. There should be no crust or distraction from its lightness. The flavour of a plain sponge should arise from good-quality eggs and the melted, browned butter. The latter gives a subtle, nutty character. The sponge should be sweet enough to authenticate itself as a dessert, but not overpoweringly so.

# BASIC GENOISE SPONGE RECIPE
MAKES TWO 8-INCH SPONGES

*30g salted butter*
*4 medium eggs*
*100g caster sugar*
*100g plain flour*

### LINE
Draw around an 8-inch tin and cut out a piece of baking paper to line the bottom. Use a little butter to stick it down. Grease the sides lightly with butter, then cover with a band of baking paper. Do not grease the baking paper. Alternatively, dust a lightly greased tin with flour, removing any excess.

### WHY
A genoise that sticks is a disaster. This is a delicate sponge that is easily torn; every care must be taken to prevent sticking. Using baking paper or coating the tin with flour is essential to avoid direct contact between the mixture and the butter, which will disrupt the fabric of the mix and cause collapsing at the sides.

### BEURRE NOISETTE
Weigh the butter into a saucepan and place this on a high heat to melt, stirring all the time, until it is a deep brown colour. To arrest the colour development, plunge the pan into a sink of cold water. Leave it to cool. This is called a 'beurre noisette' (literally 'hazelnut butter').

### WHY
When butter is burned, it gives off quite a harsh, nutty aroma and colour. Diluted into a whole cake, this is subtle but warming. The browning happens when the lactose (sugar) in the butter caramelises and the remaining milk proteins undergo Maillard (browning) reactions.

### BAIN MARIE
Into a large bowl, weigh the eggs and caster sugar. Place the bowl over a pan of simmering water, making sure there is no contact between bowl and water. Stir or whisk until the sugary eggs are just warm to the touch. This doesn't take long.

### WHY
At higher temperatures, the proteins in the eggs unfurl much easier, allowing them to capture larger volumes of gas. This is why you shouldn't use eggs straight from the fridge, because cold hampers their expanding properties. You want the temperature to be warm enough to maximise volume without cooking the eggs.

### WHISK

Using an electric or stand mixer, whisk the eggy mix on the highest speed for about 10 minutes, until it has expanded in size and doesn't look like it could possibly get any bigger. Then whisk a minute more.

### DRIZZLE

Keep whisking on a slightly slower speed and slowly pour in your cooled (but still melted) butter until combined.

### FOLD

Sift the plain flour on top of the mix (if you have a sieve). Using a large metal spoon, fold it in until completely combined. Scoop from the bottom of the bowl, bringing the subterranean mixture to the top. Turn the bowl and repeat. Once this is done, place the mix into the prepared tin.

### WHY

There is no raising agent in this cake – you've got to whisk for your life to break down the proteins in the egg, capture the air and ultimately rise the cake. You could do this by hand but it takes a while. You cannot overmix – volume will be lost in the subsequent steps and we need all we can get.

### WHY

Your butter must be cooled, or the heat will pry apart those fragile chemical bonds you've created through whisking. Equally, introducing fat too fast into a delicate structure tends to cause bad things to happen. The proteins will surround the fat (an emulsion) rather than the air (a foam). Add the butter little by little.

### WHY

The primary aim here is to preserve as much of the air you've whipped in as possible, and it is the one situation in baking where sifting flour is appropriate – it just stops the flour landing with extreme force on top of your delicate mixture. You should use a metal spoon to cut through your mix effectively without disrupting the matrix.

## THE BAKE

Genoise sponges are light, so heat penetrates them quickly. A higher baking temperature is therefore appropriate, as the heat can get through to the middle before any nasty crusts form.

For a deep cake (5cm or so), go for the safe option: 180°C/160°C fan/Gas 4 for about 20–25 minutes. For thin slivers of a cake, definitely go hotter: 200°C/180°C fan/Gas 6 for 10 minutes or less. You could even go hotter if you're feeling confident.

If your cake is deeper than 5cm, I believe you should tentatively go a bit lower (maybe by 10°C or so) and bake for a wee bit longer, but you should consider the possibility that your cake is too deep. Deep genoise sponges will never, ever hold their shape – they will concertina under their own weight.

You'll know when the sponge is done because it will spring back exuberantly when pressed. Don't press too hard, though, or you'll poke your finger right through. It should be a pale golden brown colour on top, though not as dark as a Victoria sponge. Leave it to cool in the tin and handle it gently once it's out; there's no need for a cooling rack unless you want to speed up the process.


## VARIATIONS

**DRIZZLE**   It's not just lemon drizzle cake that benefits from the addition of a sugar syrup. Boiling the juice of any citrus fruit and 100g caster sugar creates a syrup that will give a genoise an extra dimension of flavour and keep it moist for days. It's best to brush this on any cut surface of your cake, but you can just drizzle it on top too.

**FRUIT**   You can add flavour and amazing colour to a genoise by adding blitzed fresh fruit to the mix. In place of one of the eggs, add 100g puréed raspberries, cherries or blueberries (the latter work especially well). Your structure will be ever so slightly wetter, but you'll also find it beautifully moist and the perfect accompaniment to richer, sweeter fillings.

**NUTS**   Add 100g chopped nuts to the basic recipe for a nutty backbone and an extra dimension to the texture. Add them at the end with the flour. You can use ground nuts in place of half the flour for a slightly denser result, but one that is more crumbly and cakey. Hazelnuts are my favourites, but almonds are more traditional.

**CHOCOLATE**   Simply replace 35g flour with 35g cocoa powder for a perfect chocolate genoise. This works well rolled up, Swiss-roll style with whipped cream (see page 38) or chocolate ganache (see page 30). You don't even need a special tin; just use a flat-bottomed roasting tray with some baking paper shoved in.

## SUBSTITUTIONS

**FLOUR**   Your choice of flour doesn't really matter – if you have only self-raising, you can use that. If you want to use gluten-free flour, that's fine, but don't fill the tin too deep (more than 3–4cm) or you will have a squished sponge with a dense bottom. Adding ground nuts with the flour works well to give extra strength in gluten-free genoise.

**RAISING AGENT**   It's such a hideous cop-out, but you can add some baking powder if you're worried about not getting enough of a rise. Mary Berry does it, but that doesn't make it okay. Be a purist.

**EGGS**   I'm afraid I cannot recommend replacing the eggs completely. But if you've only got large eggs, weigh them out (no shells) and aim for between 180–200g of egg.

**SUGAR**   You should only use caster sugar. A mix made with granulated sugar ends up crystally and not as light, whilst icing sugar doesn't provide the level of force required to rip air holes in your egg.

**BUTTER**   You can omit the fat from the basic recipe. This will give a sponge that you simply cannot match for aeration in non-bread baking. However, the lack of butter really does affect the flavour, so you've got to make sure the fillings are prominent. Equally, fat acts as a preservative, so if you remove it your cake won't last much longer than a day.

## STORAGE

The sponge will keep for around three days at room temperature, wrapped in cling film, if you used butter. If soaked in syrup it will keep a little longer.

It will keep for a week in the fridge if wrapped and airtight. Bring to room temperature before enjoying. And if frozen, the sponge will keep indefinitely. Allow it to come to room temperature slowly. And if slicing into thin discs (see recipes), do this after freezing, not before.

# TROUBLESHOOTING

*Why has my genoise not risen?* There are a few possibilities, assuming you've used the correct ingredients and followed the basic guide. The first is that you simply haven't beaten your egg and sugar mixture enough to build the solid structure necessary to support the subsequent abuse it suffers. The second is that the butter was too hot when added, or it was added too quickly, melting through your brittle bubbles. Finally, you could have caused your mix too much stress when you folded in the flour, again smooshing your froth into non-existence.

**Why has my genoise stuck?** You didn't use the right paper (make sure it is baking paper and not greaseproof), your paper didn't cover the whole tin, or you didn't grease and flour any exposed areas.

**Why has my genoise sunk in the middle?** Believe it or not, you can have too much air in your genoise, though it's a rare occurrence. First, check the size of your eggs; if they are too big, your flour might not be able to support the structure and your genoise will sink in the middle. This is 'overegging the pudding'.

**Why is my genoise short and domed?** Very simple: you used too much flour, or you overmixed at the end, developing the gluten in the flour and getting rid of all the air you worked so hard to beat in. Only mix until the flour is *just* combined; if there are any concealed lumps, mix them in as you are pouring into the tin.

**Why is my genoise dense and flat at the bottom?** It sounds like your genoise has concertinaed under its own weight. This can happen if you make the cake too deep or if you handle it recklessly after baking. Gently remove it from the oven when it is cooked and leave to cool in the tin.

# PRALINE & CREAM GENOISE
MAKES ONE 8-INCH GENOISE SPONGE

As simple as it gets – but to many, this is the pinnacle of sponges. It is pure and it is stunning. Cream. Sponge. Nuts. No adulteration.

This is also one of the quickest cakes, start to finish, that you can make. Because of the genoise's super-light nature, it bakes and cools fast. The smaller cakes involved in this bake add to this speediness. All you need to do in between times is whip up some cream and, if you like, practise a crafty bit of sugarwork. Add any spun sugar or other caramel decoration just before serving. *(Pictured overleaf.)*

*For the sponge*
30g salted butter
4 medium eggs
100g caster sugar
100g plain flour

*For the praline*
300g roasted, blanched
   hazelnuts (or your
   favourite nut)
200g caster sugar
2 tablespoons water

*For the whipped cream*
500ml double cream
caster sugar and vanilla extract,
   to taste

1. Preheat your oven to 190°C/170°C fan/Gas 5. Line the bottom of two 8-inch cake tins with baking paper, then grease and flour the sides. If your nuts are not already roasted, place them on a tray in the oven at this point.

2. For the sponge, start by melting the butter in a pan so it has time to cool slightly. Continue heating until it goes a deep brown colour. Take this off the heat and leave to cool.

3. Into a large bowl, crack the eggs and add the sugar. Using an electric mixer, whisk for a good 5–10 minutes – your eggs should turn to a light, fragile foam. After 10 minutes, slowly drizzle in the melted, cooled butter, whisking all the time.

4. Add the flour (through a sieve if you have one), fold in until completely incorporated, and divide the mix between the two tins. Remove the hazelnuts from the oven, if roasting, and bake your cakes for 15–20 minutes, or until golden brown, light and springy and coming away from the edge of the tins. Once done, leave to cool in the tins.

5. Make the praline. This first involves making a caramel (see my guide on page 27). Into a clean pan, weigh the sugar and water. Place on a medium heat, stirring all the time to dissolve the sugar. Once dissolved, stop stirring. Bring the sugar to the boil and bubble until it turns a light golden brown colour. Place the roasted nuts on some baking paper and drizzle the caramel over the top. Leave this to cool, then smash it to smithereens. This is fun.

6. Whip the cream by hand until just coagulated, adding sugar and vanilla extract to taste (see my guide on page 38). Cover and chill.

7. Once the cakes are cooled, cut each one in half horizontally with a bread knife to make four layers. Build up the cake, spreading a good amount of cream over each layer followed by a sprinkle of shards of praline. The decoration for the top is up to you. I like to keep it simple. But you could pipe fancy patterns of cream or make a wee spun sugar nest (see page 27).

# ALTERNATIVE BIRTHDAY CAKE
## (WHISKY DRIZZLE CAKE)

MAKES ONE 9-INCH CAKE

For me, this is the perfect birthday cake because I was once baked a version of this cake on a very special birthday.

I'll admit, context did play a part (it was my 21st in fact, and just before they announced I'd won star baker in the quarter final of *Bake Off*), but I cannot thank Georgia, the home economist who made it, enough. I've made one or two wee additions – notably the whisky, without which no occasion is complete.

This cake can be made well in advance and you can use any citrus fruit. I like orange because the bitterness of the zest works especially well with the heat of the spirit.

*For the sponge*
30g salted butter
100g caster sugar
4 medium eggs
finely grated zest of 1 large
    orange
100g plain flour

*For the candied orange peel*
1 orange
100g caster sugar
100g water

*For the whisky drizzle*
100g water
juice of 1 large orange
100g caster sugar
50g whisky (roughly two
    measures), or your choice
    of spirit

1 x quantity crème pâtissière
    (see page 23)
icing sugar, for dusting

1. Preheat your oven to 180°C/160°C fan/Gas 4. Prepare a 9-inch cake tin by lining the bottom with a circle of baking paper, then greasing and flouring the sides.

2. For the sponge, melt the butter in a pan on a high heat, then continue to heat until it goes a deep brown colour. Once at this stage, remove from the heat and let it cool down.

3. Into a large bowl, weigh out the caster sugar, zest and eggs. Using an electric mixer, whisk these together for 5–10 minutes, until they form a light foam with almost stiff peaks. Slowly drizzle in the melted, cooled butter, whisking all the time, until completely incorporated.

4. Fold in the flour gently using a large metal spoon. Then pour the mix carefully into your tin, incorporating any loose flour as you do this. Place in the oven and bake for 20–25 minutes or until golden brown, light and springy. Leave to cool in the tin when it's done.

5. Whilst it's baking, make the crème pat (see page 23). If you're feeling adventurous, you could add whisky, triple sec, orange blossom water or orange zest to the mix. Cover with cling film and leave to cool in the fridge.

6. For the candied orange peel, finely slice the zest of the orange, place in a pan with the sugar and water and bring to a boil. Reduce the heat to a gentle simmer, and keep cooking until you've boiled off nearly all the water (the sugar will start to go brown) – about 10 minutes. Carefully remove the zest onto a piece of baking paper.

7. Whilst the cake's cooling, make the drizzle. Weigh all the ingredients into a pan and bring to the boil over a high heat, bubbling to evaporate the liquid. Remove the cake from the tin, slice it in half horizontally with a bread knife and pour your drizzle onto the cut side of each half.

8. Build your cake. Spoon or pipe a layer of crème pat onto one of the cake halves. Then peel and chop the flesh of one of the zested oranges (from the sponge or candied peel) and scatter this on top, before topping with the other cake. Dust with icing sugar, finishing with a pile of candied peel.

# WEE SPONGES
## WITH PASSION FRUIT CURD & ITALIAN MERINGUE
MAKES 12 MUFFIN-SIZED CAKES

If you like things light – things that make you feel like you've actually just eaten nothing at all – this recipe is for you.

This is a glorious sponge that can be made in any form. I've made it in wee cupcake cases because I believe it works well from an aesthetic perspective, but you could use it for madeleines, financiers or as a bigger cake, too. All I know is that the light sponge, sharp curd and sweet meringue make for a brilliant combination.

Although the title might make this sound daunting, this recipe is simple. There are just three processes involved: making a sponge, making a curd and making meringue, and this recipe is good practice for each.

*For the sponge*
*30g salted butter*
*100g caster sugar*
*4 medium eggs, plus 1 extra yolk*
*110g plain flour*

*For the Italian meringue*
*2 medium egg whites*
*100g caster sugar*
*25g cold water*

*For the passion fruit curd*
*5 passion fruits*
*50g unsalted butter*
*1 medium egg, plus 1 extra yolk*
*50g caster sugar*

1. Preheat your oven to 190°C/170°C fan/Gas 5. Line a 12-hole bun tin with cupcake cases.

2. For the sponge, melt the butter in a pan on a high heat, then continue to heat until it goes a deep brown colour. Once it has reached this stage, remove from the heat and let it cool down.

3. Into a large bowl, weigh out the caster sugar, eggs and yolk. Using an electric mixer, whisk these together for 5–10 minutes until they form a light foam with almost stiff peaks. Slowly drizzle in the melted, cooled butter, whisking all the time, until completely incorporated.

4. Fold in the flour gently using a large metal spoon. Then, working quickly so the air doesn't escape, scoop the mix into your cupcake cases. Place in the oven and bake for 15–20 minutes, until golden brown, light and springy. Leave to cool in the tin.

5. Whilst the cakes are baking and cooling, make the passion fruit curd. Scoop the flesh out of the passion fruits and into a pan, then add the butter, egg, yolk and sugar. Whisk everything together, then place on a medium heat and cook until the curd is noticeably thicker, stirring all the time. Pour into a jug or jar and keep in the fridge until needed.

6. To make the Italian meringue, first make sure you're familiar with the principles (see page 220). Whisk the egg whites in a clean bowl to stiff peaks. Weigh the caster sugar and water into a pan. Place on a medium heat and stir until the sugar has dissolved, then stop stirring and bring to a boil. Continue to the soft ball stage – 118°C on a thermometer, or exactly 30 seconds of furious boiling. Slowly drizzle this mixture into your meringue, whisking on the highest speed all the time. Your Italian meringue is ready.

7. Build the cakes. Drizzle a heaped teaspoon of passion fruit curd over each cake. Load your Italian meringue into a piping bag with a nozzle of your choice, and pipe a swirl onto the top of each cake, before browning with a blowtorch or drizzling with more curd. These will keep in or out of the fridge in an airtight container for several days.

# CUCUMBER, STRAWBERRY & MINT FRAISIER

MAKES ONE 9-INCH FRAISIER

The fraisier is a stunning-looking but simple-to-make cake that involves a genoise sponge sandwiching a layer of strawberries and crème pâtissière. Both layers are usually soaked in a light lemon syrup to help them maintain moisture. You may see mint worked into a fraisier in any traditional establishment; strawberry and mint is a well-honed combination. But cucumber? Am I mad? I don't actually like cucumber very much. But in this, I just can't get enough of it. It works so well with the strawberries and the mint that it seems to cause an epiphany with every bite and makes you want more straight away. *(Pictured overleaf.)*

Serve with a strawberry mojito (oh, wait, that's where I got the idea...).

*For the sponge*
*30g salted butter*
*100g caster sugar*
*4 medium eggs*
*100g plain flour*

*For the crème mousseline*
*1 x quantity crème pâtissière*
*(see page 23)*
*125g softened, unsalted butter*

*For the drizzle*
*juice of ½ lemon*
*50g caster sugar*
*2 large punnets of strawberries*
*1 cucumber*
*a handful of fresh mint*

1. Preheat your oven to 180°C/160°C fan/Gas 4. Line the bottom of a 9-inch springform cake tin with baking paper, then grease and flour the sides or line them with more baking paper.

2. For the sponge, melt the butter in a pan on a medium heat, then continue to heat until it goes a deep brown colour. Once it has reached this stage, remove from the heat and let it cool down.

3. Into a large bowl, weigh out the sugar and eggs. Using an electric mixer, whisk these together for about 10 minutes until expanded and almost stiff peaks. Once you've mixed as much as you can bear, slowly add the melted and cooled butter until completely incorporated.

4. Fold in the flour with a large metal spoon, then scoop the mix into your prepared tin and place in the oven to bake for approximately 25–30 minutes, or until well-risen, golden brown and springy (but fragile) to touch. Leave to cool in the tin.

5. Whilst the sponge is baking and cooling, make the crème pat (see page 23). Cover with cling film and leave to cool in the fridge. Once it's chilled, whisk it using an electric mixer, adding chunks of the soft butter little by little to make a light mousse. This is a crème mousseline. Scoop it into a piping bag and leave in the fridge.

6. Make the drizzle by mixing the lemon juice and sugar together in a pan and placing on a high heat. As soon as it starts to boil, remove from the heat. Remove the cooled sponges from the tin, then slice in half horizontally with a bread knife; you want the top half slightly thinner than the bottom half. Then brush the drizzle equally onto the cut-side of each half.

7. This is the tricky bit. Cut a long rectangle of baking paper, about 6 inches deep. It should stretch around the sides of the tin you baked the sponge in. Place the parchment inside the tin, using a little butter to help it stick to the sides if you need to. Then replace the bottom half of your cake in the tin.

8. Cut a handful of the strawberries in half and remove the stalks, then line these up, upside down, around the edge of the cake with the cut-side facing the paper. Cut your cucumber into very thin slices, and cover the remaining area of the cake with a thin layer of cucumber. Onto the cucumber, pipe a layer of crème mousseline. Dice some strawberries and scatter these on top of the layer of crème. You should have used up at least half of your strawberries by this point. Then roll 10–12 small fresh mint leaves between your hands and sprinkle these on top of the strawberries.

9. Now, use your piping bag of crème mousseline to fill in all the gaps around the edge and between each half-strawberry. You should then fill in the whole cake up to the level of the tips of the halved strawberries. Finally, top with the other layer of sponge, cut-side down.

10. To decorate, spread the remaining crème mousseline on top of the cake to help the fruit and veg stick. Slice the remaining strawberries thinly and the cucumber very thinly. Lay a line of strawberries like fallen dominoes around the edge of the cake, then do the same with the cucumber, alongside the strawberries but pointing in the other direction. Repeat until you reach the middle. Finish with a few whole strawberries and plenty of fresh mint leaves. For a more professional finish, make a glaze by boiling any remaining strawberries with some caster sugar and brushing this on top. Carefully lift off the tin.

# BLUEBERRY PIZZA

MAKES ONE 12-INCH PIZZA

This recipe exists because of a wee boy called Elliott. My editor, the lovely Sarah Lavelle, is his mum.

Elliott invited me round for 'dinner' once during his first year at primary school. He was turning the house into a pop-up restaurant, achieving his lifelong ambition. I was thrilled to read 'blueberry pizza' on the blackboard menu.

The experience at Elliott's restaurant was definitely 5-star (the sherry he served was especially excellent), but there was one disappointment: there wasn't actually any blueberry pizza. I promised we'd make one together next time I visited. And this is it.

Despite involving a genoise sponge, three different types of superheated sugar and a blowtorch, this is an excellent recipe to bake with kids. Seriously. It's healthy (well, it involves fruit, and you can use low-fat custard . . . ), fast and fun. You can take care of the potentially scalding stuff whilst the kids do all the whisking.

*For the sponge*
*50g caster sugar*
*2 medium eggs*
*finely grated zest of 1 lemon*
*50g plain flour*

*For the jam*
*200g blueberries*
*(frozen are best)*
*100g caster sugar*

*For the drizzle*
*juice of 1 lemon*
*(from the zested fruit above)*
*100g caster sugar*

*1 x quantity crème anglaise*
*(see page 24),*
*or use shop-bought custard*
*50g flaked almonds*
*caster sugar, for sprinkling*
*fresh blueberries, to finish*

1. Preheat your oven 200°C/180°C fan/Gas 6. Line the bottom of the largest tin you own (I used a 12-inch springform tin) with baking paper, grease the sides and dust with plenty of flour.

2. Make the custard following the instructions on page 24, unless you're using shop-bought.

3. For the sponge, weigh out the sugar, eggs and grated zest into a bowl. Using an electric mixer, whisk these together for at least 10 minutes until light, fluffy and almost stiff peaks. You can get the kids to do this.

4. Fold in the flour gently with a metal spoon until combined. Pour the mix into your prepared tin and spread it out evenly. Bake for 10 minutes on the middle shelf, or until light and springy.

5. Whilst the sponge is baking, make the jam. Put the frozen blueberries and sugar into a pan on a medium heat to melt the blueberries, then continue heating until they've broken down and

the mixture is boiling. Reduce the heat and simmer for 5 minutes to thicken, then remove from the heat and set aside.

6. Once the cake is ready, leave it to cool in the tin whilst you make the drizzle. Put the lemon juice and caster sugar into a pan on a high heat and stir until the sugar has dissolved. Bring to the boil, and as soon as it is bubbling furiously, remove from the heat. Use a skewer to make little holes in the cake, then spread about half the drizzle on top with a pastry brush.

7. Transfer your drizzled cake onto a pizza board, then 'upcycle' the baking paper it was baked on by folding it and placing the flaked almonds on top. Return the pan with the remaining drizzle back to the heat (medium) and simmer until golden brown. Pour this onto the nuts and leave to set.

8. Spread the jam on top of your 'pizza base', almost to the edge. Then spread a thick layer of custard on top and sprinkle the whole thing with sugar. If desired, blowtorch the top for a browned, melted-cheese-style effect.

9. Scatter the fresh blueberries on top, and blowtorch these quickly to give them a shine (you could glaze them, but the former is quicker). Chop the almond praline into shards and lay these on top. Your pizza is now ready to enjoy.

# CHOCOLATE CREAM ROLL
MAKES ONE LARGE CHOCOLATE ROLL

This is a basic chocolate genoise with a cream filling. Specifically for this recipe, I've simplified the method to make it extra-easy, thus fulfilling its role as a last-minute dessert.

If you want to make something that's true to the miniature Cadbury classic, fill it with marshmallow rather than cream (see Swiss meringue, page 223).

*For the sponge*
*75g caster sugar*
*3 medium eggs, at room*
*temperature*
*50g plain flour*
*25g cocoa powder*

*For the whipped cream*
*300ml double cream*
*caster sugar and vanilla extract,*
*to taste*
*200g good dark chocolate,*
*optional*

1. Preheat your oven to 200°C/180°C fan/Gas 6. Unless you've got a Swiss roll tin, line a roasting tray with a double layer of foil so you can lift out your cake once baked. Draw around the bottom of your tin onto some baking paper, cut this out and line the tray. Grease the foil at the sides and cover with flour, removing any excess.

2.  For the sponge, weigh the sugar and eggs into a bowl. Beat with an electric mixer until super-light and fluffy – this will take a long time of solid beating. You could do this over a pan of simmering water for greater volume, but it's not essential.

3.  Add the flour and cocoa powder (through a sieve if you have one) and fold in with a metal spoon until your mix is consistent and smooth. Take care not to force out any of the air you've incorporated. Pour the mix into your prepared tray, spreading it out flat, and bake for 10–12 minutes until puffed up and springy. When it's done, immediately remove from the tray and turn upside down onto a surface to cool.

4.  Whilst the cake is cooling, whip the cream by hand until just coagulated, adding sugar and vanilla to taste (see page 38).

5.  When the cake has cooled, remove the baking paper (it should come away easily). Spread the cream over the cake, then roll it up carefully but tightly, placing the seam on the bottom. You could simply dust with cocoa powder and serve at this point, but I like to cover it in chocolate.

6.  Break three-quarters of the chocolate into chunks and zap in a bowl in the microwave for 15 seconds at a time, stirring after each burst. Whilst that's melting, chop the rest of the chocolate finely. Once the main batch of chocolate has melted, stir in the rest until melted and combined (see my guide on pages 28–30). Drizzle over the cake and leave to set at room temperature.

OPPOSITE: BASIC BROWNIES

# BROWNIE

# BROWNIE

A brownie is a dense cake made with melted butter and chocolate. Compared to a Victoria sponge, it has a low flour content, making it unable to support a light and intricate structure. It is a thing of condensed beauty.

Brownies are awesome. If asked to bake something, the basic recipe below is my fundamental go-to dessert, bake-sale contribution and competition prize. I have the quantities engrained in my memory and recommend you learn them too.

## THE IDEAL BROWNIE

My test of any chocolate dessert is simple: eat some of the chocolate you baked with. If you'd rather have the chocolate than the brownie, you've failed.

A perfect brownie should be served at room temperature. It should be of even height throughout, without noticeable crust at the sides. If baked without fruit, it should have a clean, shiny surface that cracks on cutting. The texture should be dense, but it should not ooze or flow – it should be cooked through. However, it should be very moist and slicing should be at least treacherous. The addition of fruit, nuts and chocolate chips is acceptable.

A brownie should never be overly sweet – whether made with white, dark or milk chocolate, the backbone should be the chocolate itself; too much sugar will detract from the taste. Any additional flavours should complement this. It should be extremely rich, but not so as to limit enjoyment. Fruit and nuts may aid in cutting through the richness.

## BASIC BROWNIE RECIPE
### MAKES ENOUGH FOR AN 8-INCH SQUARE TIN

*250g good-quality dark chocolate*
*250g salted butter*
*3 eggs, plus an extra yolk*
*300g caster sugar*
*60g plain flour (or gluten-free)*
*60g cocoa powder*
*a handful of nuts, chocolate chips or berries*

### STUFF

Stuff a ripped off square of baking paper into a brownie tin; an 8-inch square tin is about right for this recipe.

### WHY

Baking paper is awesome. There's no greasing to worry about – this stuff is siliconised to prevent sticking. Rough edges are part of a brownie's charm; do not cut the baking paper to size.

### MELT

Into a small bowl, weigh the chocolate and salted butter. Place the bowl in a microwave or above a pan of boiling water and melt these together.

### WHY

Microwave isn't a dirty word. It is an extremely gentle, even way of melting chocolate and it can be used for expert tempering. The chocolate shouldn't be so hot as to scramble the impending eggs.

### SWEET EGGS

Whilst the chocolate and butter are melting, crack your eggs and egg yolk into a large bowl and add the sugar. Whisk these together, just to combine.

### WHY

At this stage, you have two options. You can whisk for your life and create loads of air, resulting in brownies that rise up then collapse after taking them out of the oven. Or you can be gentle – the brownies won't rise as much, but they won't fall as much either. The latter option gives you a better shine on top, as the surface goes through less stress when baking.

## COMBINE

Add your melted chocolate mixture into your eggy mixture and combine.

## FOLD AND TRANSFER

Add the flour, cocoa powder and any nuts or chips. Fold them in with a large metal spoon, gently bringing the mixture from the bottom up to the top. Turn your bowl and repeat. Pour your mix into your prepared tin, scatter over any berries and bake as below.

## WHY

As in the previous step, overmixing here will introduce too much air and you'll end up with matt brownies – the worst kind.

## WHY

Adding cocoa powder increases the bitterness and the richness of the brownies. Fold in as gently as you can to prevent gluten development and thus doughy brownies. Obviously, if you've used gluten-free flour, indulge in a rare bit of reckless final mixing.

# THE BAKE

Baking brownies is easy. You've just got to take it low and slow.

Set your oven to 160°C/140°C fan/Gas 3 for 1–2-inch-deep brownies, using an 8-inch square tin. You'll want to bake them for a good long time – approximately 40–50 minutes. Knowing whether they are baked can be difficult, for a skewer may never come out clean. They should, however, not be wobbly when shaken. Another tip is to listen to them – if they are singing and popping and otherwise making noises, they need a wee bit longer. If you slice them later on and they ooze, increase the baking time when you next make them. For super-thick brownies or those with moist fillings, turn your oven down by 20°C and bake for even longer – I've often had brownies in for up to an hour and a half if I've been generous with my ingredients and filling. For faster brownies, divide them between tins to make them thinner and go up 20°C – they'll be done in 20 minutes easily.

To avoid that dreaded crusty dryness around the edges of perfectly baked brownies, try this: when you are satisfied the brownies are cooked, take them out of the oven and gently plunge the tin into a sink filled about an inch full with cold water. This stops the edges overcooking even after the brownies are out of the oven, and regulates the temperature throughout.

Never serve brownies chilled. They are best enjoyed straight after cooling.

# VARIATIONS

**CHUNKS**   I especially like berries, as they cut through the richness and mean you can polish off a whole tray with ease. I also tend to chuck blueberries, blackberries or raspberries on top at the end, simply for aesthetic purposes. Otherwise, any sort of nuts (my favourites are hazelnut and macadamia nuts) and chocolate chunks work too.

**BLONDIES**   Replace dark chocolate with white chocolate and replace cocoa powder with flour. Cut down the fat and sugar by 50g each to account for the higher content of both in the chocolate. Macadamia nuts work particularly well in blondies.

**MAYONNAISE**   My beautiful friend and co-*Bake Off*er John Whaite swears by adding mayonnaise to brownies. The taste is swamped by the chocolate, so don't worry about it coming through. But it adds a great moistness and reduces the richness slightly. Like adding a mixture of egg and oil would, if you think about it.

**THE NIGELLA METHOD**   Say you like your brownies a bit less chocolatey and a bit more … gooey. Ramp up the butter (100g extra will do – more if you like) and omit the cocoa. Extra nuts here will work, too.

**CHEESECAKE BROWNIES**   Mix together 150g full-fat cream cheese, an egg and 75g caster sugar. Marble this mixture into your brownie mix once it is in the tin.

**COFFEE**   Add a shot of espresso to the mix; there is no noticeable coffee flavour, just extra chocolatiness.

## SUBSTITUTIONS

**FLOUR**   Gluten-free flours are always excellent, directly replacing the plain flour. Self-raising varieties work as well. The resulting texture will be a little different, but no worse.

**EGGS**   You can replace with vegan substitutes. If you want vegan brownies, replace the butter with the same amount of oil, the eggs with water (200g), and bake as in the basic recipe.

**SUGAR**   The sugar can be subbed for all kinds of brown or white sugar with success. You cannot omit it, though. And you can't use sweeteners, you masochist.

**CHOCOLATE**   White chocolate and milk chocolate both work; just cut down the butter and the sugar a tad. Not a fan of chocolate? Try substituting peanut butter (or any nut butter).

## STORAGE

Brownies keep well. Store at room temperature in a tin, wrapped in cling film, for up to four days.

They do freeze well, but they cannot be warmed up quickly. To freeze, wrap the whole slab (paper and all) in cling film and place back in the tin. Freeze overnight. The next day, remove the tin and return the brownies to the freezer; this stops them becoming deformed.

# TROUBLESHOOTING

*Why are my brownies raw in the middle?* Turn down your oven and bake them for longer. If they actively flow from the centre when sliced you could need anywhere upwards of 20 minutes extra. If they just gently ooze, try another 10 minutes next time. If the sides hold their structure but the bake is fairly unsliceable, that's just brownies. They're awesome, aren't they?

*Why are my brownies dry?* Either your recipe uses too much flour (unlikely if you've used mine), you've weighed it out wrong, or you've baked them for too long. Again, if they're only just cooked in the middle but dry at the sides, bake lower and slower.

*Why are my brownies unbearably rich?* It could be that you just can't handle my brownies – cut out the cocoa and add some fruit and nuts; this will help. Otherwise, check the cocoa content of your dark chocolate – don't go much above 70 percent and definitely don't hit 80 percent.

*Why are my brownies tough or doughy?* Again, you could have added too much flour, but it's more likely that you've just overmixed at the end. If you're certain you haven't, try adding some baking powder next time.

*Why are my brownies dry at the sides?* Next time, bake at a lower temperature for longer, and as soon as they are out of the oven, put your tin in a bath of cold water. This halts the cooking process at the edges almost immediately and prevents drying.

# THE RICHEST BROWNIE

MAKES ONE 8-INCH SANDWICH CAKE

This is the richest brownie I have yet imagined, though I'm sure you could do better. You should try.

This is one for fellow chocolate obsessives. It is based on the exceedingly rich basic brownie recipe on page 84, but made in two thin layers. Then chocolate ganache is added. Then it's sliced and covered in melted chocolate. Then covered in cocoa.

I hear the cries of the carried-away to add additional chocolate chips into the brownie mix, but this isn't a good idea from a chocolate snobbery point of view. Chocolate that's been through the oven is fine, but isn't tempered. If you're ever struggling with the dilemma, 'Should I put chocolate *in* it or *on* it?' then the answer is nearly always the latter. (*Pictured overleaf.*)

*250g salted butter*
*250g good-quality dark*
  *chocolate*
*3 eggs, plus an extra yolk*
*300g caster sugar*
*60g plain flour (or gluten-free)*
*60g cocoa powder*

*For the ganache*
*200g double cream*
*200g dark chocolate*

*For the topping*
*200g dark chocolate*
*cocoa powder, for dusting*

1. Preheat your oven to 160°C/140°C fan/Gas 3 and line two 7-inch cake tins with baking paper. Just stuff it in as neatly as you can, so that it's easy to lift out.

2. Melt the butter and chocolate in the microwave, or in a bowl over a pan of simmering water. Whilst that's melting away, whisk the eggs, yolk and caster sugar together in a large bowl until combined. When your chocolate's melted, whisk it into your eggy mix.

3. Add the flour and cocoa then fold in to combine. Divide the mix equally between your tins and bake for about 30 minutes or so. You don't want your brownies gooey or uncooked; they must be especially set for they are going to be cleanly sliced. A skewer should come out clean. Leave them to cool in the tin.

4. Whilst your brownies are cooling, make the ganache (see my guide on page 30). Place the double cream in a pan over a medium heat, stirring regularly. Whilst that's heating, break the chocolate into small chunks and place it in a bowl. Once your cream is boiling, pour this onto the chocolate and stir them together until well combined. Leave to cool in the fridge.

5. To build your dessert, place a layer of brownie on a flat plate or board covered with a sheet of baking paper. Spread all your ganache in a thick layer on top, right to the edge (if it's too soft, put it in the freezer to firm up). Add your other brownie layer on top.

6. For the topping, break three-quarters of the chocolate into chunks and zap in the microwave for 15 seconds at a time, stirring after each burst. During the bursts, chop your final quarter of chocolate finely. Once the main batch of chocolate is completely melted, stir in the chopped until combined. (See my guide to melting chocolate on pages 28–30.)

7. Drizzle your melted chocolate liberally over your brownie-cake and leave it to set at room temperature. Finally, dust with cocoa powder to finish. This can be kept in the fridge for several days without consequence, but let it come back to room temperature before serving.

# MACADAMIA & RASPBERRY BLONDIES
## MAKES ENOUGH FOR ONE 8-INCH SQUARE TIN

If I'm honest, I often find blondies a bit much, and am not that big a fan of white chocolate in general. But here's an example where it really shines. Macadamias are quite dry, brittle nuts that contrast with the slight gumminess of a baked blondie, and raspberries are the ultimate way of cutting through the richness.

I'd give this a go whether you're sceptical of white chocolate or its biggest fan. This will please both parties. (*Pictured overleaf.*)

*200g salted butter*
*250g good-quality white*
   *chocolate*
*3 eggs, plus an extra yolk*
*250g caster sugar*

*100g plain flour*
   *(or gluten-free)*
*100g macadamia nuts,*
   *roughly chopped*
*1 punnet of fresh raspberries*

1. Preheat your oven to 160°C/140°C fan/Gas 3. Stuff a ripped-off square of baking paper into an 8-inch square tin.

2. Melt the butter and chocolate in the microwave, or in a bowl over a pan of simmering water. Whilst that's melting, whisk the eggs, yolk and caster sugar together in a large bowl until combined.

3. Once your butter and chocolate are just melted, add them to your egg and sugar mixture. Whisk to combine. Finally, add the flour and nuts, folding them into the mix with a large spoon until just incorporated.

4. Transfer to your lined tin and scatter (or arrange) your fresh raspberries on top – when the brownies rise in the oven, the berries will be more enshrouded. Bake for 40–50 minutes on a middle shelf, depending on how squidgy or formed you like your blondies.

ABOVE: MACADAMIA & RASPBERRY BLONDIES                    OPPOSITE: PEANUT BUTTER BROWNIES

# PEANUT BUTTER BROWNIES
## MAKES ENOUGH FOR ONE 8-INCH SQUARE TIN

This recipe was inspired by the delightful Rachel Allen, who I believe created or at least propagated this simple method of making a brownie-like dessert. When I complimented her on her recipe, she recommended I didn't bake them for any school fairs, because she had been knocked back due to the presence of peanuts in the past. Fair advice. Still, these are great to make in a hurry.

This version is a little different to hers, of course. After much experimentation, I found peanut butter works so much better with dark chocolate than white. You should ideally use crunchy peanut butter, but also add some extra peanuts too. Try to get the unsalted variety, though salted ones that have been washed and dried will be fine. (*Pictured on previous page.*)

*100g softened, unsalted butter*
*150g crunchy peanut butter*
*150g caster sugar*
*1 egg, beaten*
*1 teaspoon vanilla extract*

*100g self-raising flour*
*50g unsalted peanuts*
*100g dark chocolate, chopped*

1. Preheat your oven to 170°C/150°C fan/Gas 3. Stuff a ripped-off square of baking paper into an 8-inch square tin.

2. In a large bowl, beat the butter, peanut butter and sugar together until paste-like. There is no need to cream as you would for a cake.

3. Add the egg and vanilla and beat until combined. Again, there is no need to develop air.

4. Add the flour, peanuts and chopped chocolate, stirring gently to combine. Dollop the mixture into your cake tin and spread out to the edges, for it should be quite tough.

5. Bake in the oven for 25–30 minutes or until golden brown on top and moderately resistant when pressed. A skewer inserted should come out clean.

# CARAMEL CHOCOLATE FONDANT
## MAKES 6 RAMEKINS

An awesome dessert. The chocolate fondant is not something you want to press down upon and find it springs back at you. You want it raw and as gooey as possible.

Yes, it's in the brownie section. That's because this is made more like a brownie than any other cake – honestly, it's dead easy. You can even keep them for months in the freezer, in their moulds and ready to bake and everything. My one tip here is to be liberal when greasing your ramekins or bowls, for any sticking will ruin the look of your dessert.

You can miss out the caramel to make this a plain and pure version. Other variations include adding chopped nuts through your fondant, as with brownies. You can also add orange zest into your mix, then serve with whipped cream flavoured with a few drops of orange blossom water.

1 x quantity easy caramel
   sauce (see page 28)
150g salted butter, plus extra
   for greasing
150g dark chocolate
150g caster sugar

3 medium eggs, plus 3 egg yolks
   (don't waste the whites, make
   meringues or macarons)
100g plain flour
50g cocoa powder,
   plus extra for dusting
ice cream, to serve

1. First, make the easy caramel sauce, if using (see page 28). Place this into ice cube moulds and freeze.

2. Heavily grease your ramekins (or a deep ovenproof dish if making a large fondant). And I mean heavily – loads of butter, please. Then dust each one with cocoa powder, coating the sides fully and passing any excess onto the next ramekin. Put these in the fridge to chill.

3. Melt the butter and chocolate together in a microwave, or in a bowl over a pan of simmering water. Whilst they're melting, whisk your sugar, eggs and yolks in a bowl until combined.

4. Add your chocolate mixture into your eggy mixture and whip together. Then add the flour and cocoa powder and fold in gently until combined. Your mix is now complete. Divide it between your prepared moulds, add a caramel ice cube into each (so that it is just covered) and place in the fridge for at least half an hour (an hour if it's one big fondant). You can freeze them at this point for up to a month. There's no need to thaw, just bake from frozen.

5. Whilst they're in the fridge, preheat your oven to 200°C/180°C fan/Gas 6. When the fondants have cooled, place them on a baking tray and bake for about 10 minutes – you want a light crust to have formed on top when you press. If not, bake another 2 minutes, no more. If you've made a big one, you want to bake for at least 20 minutes.

6. You might need to loosen the fondants at the side before plating up – do this gently so they don't fall apart. They should just tip out. If they don't, very gently pry them out. Serve immediately, with ice cream.

# MUFFIN

# MUFFIN

If you can bake a good muffin, you're sorted. It should be a simple ask, but some crimes committed by near masterful muffin-makers make me sad. Thus I present this chapter on the US-style muffin. For the yeasted, griddled English muffin, see that other book, *Brilliant Bread*.

A muffin is a quick, domed bread (or cake, depending on your definition). It is sized for individual portions and risen using baking powder or bicarb. It has a variety of legitimate forms: large and small; sweet and savoury; cased and uncased. Muffins are made without the charade of cakes or sponges – most recipes involve mixing all the ingredients together gently in one stage.

Often given a bad name by large tax-dodging coffee corporations for their vast calorie counts, a muffin can be one of the healthiest bakes out there. They're carby, for sure, but I'd hope we're all getting over that low-carb-diet fad by now. The sugar is adjustable and never all that high anyway, egg inclusion is nominal and poly-unsaturated oils are used rather than butter for moistness and longevity.

It may go against the rules of logic to leave lumps in your mixture, but you see the results of your restraint if you do. Once you've got the knack, you'll be hooked. These are healthy, fast and truly delicious. And they freeze excellently.

## THE IDEAL MUFFIN

The ideal muffin should have a gradual dome from edge to edge. The size can vary. The colour can also vary, from a golden brown to dark, depending on the ingredients. It should be springy but not too resilient. It should break apart easily if prised.

Any fillings should be distributed evenly and not in such quantities as to affect the integral structure of the muffin. It may be iced, but usually isn't. An overly crisp, tough or thick crust is undesirable; a cracked crust is acceptable.

On tasting, the texture should be moist but not sludgy enough to cling to the top of your mouth. Overall, they should be light and moreish, well balanced and a perfect accompaniment to hot beverages. The raising agent should not be detectable.

## BASIC MUFFIN RECIPE
MAKES 12 MUFFIN-SIZED MUFFINS

*250g plain flour*
*3 level teaspoons baking powder*
*a pinch of salt*
*A couple of handfuls of the*
*filling of your choice: berries,*
*chocolate chips, dried fruit,*
*nuts, etc.*

*1 egg*
*200g milk (any sort)*
*100g sunflower oil*
*100g caster sugar*

### GREASE

Prepare the muffin cases, if using; make sure your cases are size appropriate to your tins. Alternatively, grease your tins, right down to the very corners. Use your fingers for butter or a brush for oil.

### WHY

Sticking is a common occurrence and a stuck muffin is one that cannot be prised out easily. Oil acts as a lubricant to stop this happening. Paper muffin cases are not structurally strong, and need support up their sides; use a proper muffin tin.

### DRY

Into a bowl, weigh out the flour, baking powder, salt and any filling. Toss everything together to coat the filling. If you're using any spices, zests or seeds, add them at this point and stir in gently.

### WHY

For consistent, even results, make sure the raising agent and salt are completely mixed in. You want to coat your fruit or filling in the dry ingredients to stop them sinking to the bottom during the bake – the flour will keep the surrounding mix firm and stable and absorb any initial water released by the fruit during the bake.

### WET

Into another bowl, weigh out the egg, milk, oil and sugar. Mix everything together to distribute evenly.

### WHY

Please, please weigh your wet ingredients, if you can. This is far more accurate than volume measuring and will lead to more consistent results. The mixing distributes everything for consistency and will incorporate some air into the mix for greater rise in the oven. It is generally accepted that you cannot overmix at this stage.

## LUMPY

Add your dry ingredients to your
wet. Fold everything together slowly
and gently until you cannot see any
bare flour and don't suspect there's
any lurking beneath. The mixture
should still be lumpy.

## WHY

Overmixing is the biggest mistake in
muffin-making. As in any bake, this
causes the development of gluten
and thus the texture becomes
tough, bready and often dry. Don't
worry about the lumps; when the
mix heats up, everything should
even out in consistency. If any flour
appears when scooping, you can just
mix it in.

## DIVIDE

Scoop your mix into your cases or
tins as evenly as possible using two
dessertspoons. Try to distribute the
filling equally, by placing a little
in each case then topping up as
appropriate.

## WHY

If the mix isn't divided evenly, the
larger muffins will take longer to
cook, and the smaller ones will dry
out. It may seem silly to stress that
the filling should be distributed
equally, but it's important. I've
often ended up with some muffins
so packed with melted berries that
they disintegrate on cooling, whilst
others in the same bake have no
fruit at all.

## THE BAKE

The depth of the muffins should be taken into account when baking. I'd try 190°C/170°C fan/ Gas 5 the first time and adjust from there. A big, super-deep, Texan-style muffin will take a good 30–35 minutes, whereas a wee muffin will be done in 15 minutes. There's going to be a degree of experimentation – everyone's oven is different and everyone's idea of what constitutes a single serving is different. Fruit will protract the baking time significantly.

You don't need to stick in skewers to check that they are done. Just press down on them gently with your thumb or a finger and watch to see if they spring back. If they do, convincingly and with some vigour, your muffins are cooked. If there is any delay or you leave any indent, give them another 3–4 minutes and check again.


## VARIATIONS

CHOCOLATE  Chocolate muffins can be made easily by adding 4 tablespoons (about 50g) of cocoa powder to your muffin recipe with the dry ingredients, cutting down your flour by about half that much (25g). Chocolate works particularly well if you replace the milk with natural yoghurt or buttermilk. Chocolate chips also work well. Obviously.

BANANA  Squish about 3 medium-sized, overripe bananas and add these to your wet ingredients. Cut down your liquid by around 50g.

FRUITS/BERRIES  Frozen fruits work particularly well. Halve the weight of your flour and add the same weight of fruit. Alternatively, just add it by the punnet or the handful. As a rule, one standard punnet is always the right quantity of fruit to add.

VEGETABLES  Grated vegetables such as carrot, parsnip, courgette, aubergine and beetroot (especially with chocolate), all add great moisture and flavour to your muffins and cakes. Simply grate about 300g of the peeled veg and fold straight into the basic recipe at the end of step 4. You might want to dab the grated veg with kitchen paper first to remove any excessive moisture.

FUNKY  This just means replacing your milk with a cultured or fermented variety. Yoghurt, buttermilk and soured cream all add amazing flavour to your muffins. Experiment with different combinations, and if you're lacking something, don't hesitate to substitute radically. Muffins are hard to ruin.

SECRET CENTRE  Your secret centre can be anything from jam to crème pat to ganache. My favourite is cheesecake: mix 100g full-fat cream cheese and 50g of caster sugar and chill. Fill your tins half full with your normal muffin mixture, scoop on a dollop of cheesecake mix, then cover with more muffin mix.

## SUBSTITUTIONS

FLOUR   Plain flour and baking powder can be replaced with self-raising flour. Gluten-free flour can be substituted 1:1 for plain flour, though you should consider doubling your eggs and reducing your milk slightly to help with the rise. Gluten-free flour works especially well with bananas.

BAKING POWDER   In recipes containing acidic ingredients, such as sour fruits, chocolate and banana, you can just about get away with using bicarb only instead of baking powder.

SUGAR   Any type of sugar can be used successfully. Do not use sweeteners, however; you'd struggle to find evidence for the benefit.

MILK   Milk can be replaced with just about any liquid. I like other dairy liquids, but you can use water, beer, fruit juices . . . anything.

FAT   You can miss out the fat altogether, but try not to. The muffins will last about a day.

EGG   Vegan muffins are easy to make: just replace the egg with 4 mashed bananas and the milk with a dash of water.


## STORAGE

Muffins should ideally be enjoyed on the day of baking. If not, don't serve them to your friends any later than the day after. If they do go a bit dry, some people like to microwave them to soften.

Like most baking, muffins freeze well. I tend to bag them in a supermarket plastic bag, twirl the top and chuck them in the freezer (you should probably use a food-safe plastic freezer bag). They defrost very quickly, but you can use the microwave to speed things up.

# TROUBLESHOOTING

*Why are my muffins dry?* Two things make muffins dry from the outset: too much flour and overbaking. Make sure your muffins aren't baked to excess by checking them every 5 minutes or so. If you find you consistently bake dry muffins, try adding an extra glug of oil or a bit more milk. And eat them within a day: it could be that your muffins are stale.

*Why do they rise in the middle but not at the sides?* Simple: too much baking powder. All baking powders react differently, so if the quantity above is too much, cut back a bit. Adding a bit more flour can also help make your muffins evenly dome-shaped.

*Why are they flat on top?* Are they a bit cupcake-shaped? That means either your oven isn't hot enough, or you've got too much liquid in your mix. Add a bit more flour and turn up the oven by 20°C.

*Why are they raw in the middle and burnt on the outside?* Your oven is too hot. Turn it down and increase the cooking time. You risk forming a crust and the muffins becoming dry if baked too long, however, so check them regularly. Don't worry about opening the oven door; just don't poke them if they're still obviously wet.

*Why haven't my muffins risen?* Baking powder and self-raising flour go off if they're left sitting in the back of the cupboard for ages. If this is the case, go and buy some more.

# 'SUMMER FRUIT' MUFFINS

MAKES 12 MEDIUM MUFFINS

When I was about 13, I went through a phase when I baked a batch of these every single week for well over a year. They're tasty and easy to make, but most importantly, you should have most of the ingredients lying around. And if you don't, you will for next time.

I tend to use tinned 'summer fruits' because that's all I could ever find at my local shop, but these work equally well with frozen mixed berries. The tinned variety tend to break apart when you fold them in, but I like this. It adds colour and flavour to the muffin and makes it almost puddingy if you scoff them straight from the oven.

The slight acidity of the berries means that you should reduce the quantity of baking powder and replace this quantity with bicarb – you should then have fairly equal quantities of acid and alkali to react together to cause the rise of the muffins in the oven.

400g tin of summer berries
   (or a packet frozen berries)
100g caster sugar
a pinch of salt
1 egg
100g milk (any sort)

100g natural yoghurt
100g sunflower oil
250g plain flour
1½ level teaspoons
   baking powder
½ teaspoon bicarbonate of soda

1. Preheat your oven to 190°C/170°C fan/Gas 5. Grease a 12-hole muffin tin with plenty of butter or oil, or line your tin with muffin cases.

2. Drain your tin of berries (if using), keeping the syrup. I generally let the liquid drain through the almost-opened tin.

3. Into a large bowl, weigh the sugar, salt, egg, milk, yoghurt and oil. Whisk them all together until completely combined.

4. Add the flour, baking powder and bicarb on top, mixing the raising agents into the flour a little with your fingers so they are evenly distributed. Then, using a large rigid spoon, fold everything together until it is nearly combined – there should still be bits of flour visible.

5. Add the drained fruit and, with just a couple of turns, finish off the mixing and distribute the fruit. This is so as you don't crush the fruit and overmix the dough. Your mix shouldn't have any visible flour now, but should be lumpy.

6. Spoon your mix into your tin and, depending on size, bake for about 20–30 minutes, turning the oven down if they're browning too fast. It's best not to open the oven door too much, but a sneak peek now and again won't do any harm. When done, leave to cool in the tin for at least half an hour before removing.

7. As an optional flourish, place the reserved syrup in a pan and bring to the boil. Reduce until very thick and syrupy (a few minutes). Then brush onto your baked muffins.

# YOGHURT MUFFINS

MAKES 12 MEDIUM MUFFINS

Yoghurt muffins . . . Just yoghurt? Just yoghurt.

The first time I had that conversation, it was regarding gelato. In Italy, you'll notice that one of the most touted flavours is yoghurt. And it isn't some kind of 'fro-yo' that exists for obese Americans to feel good about themselves; the best is rich and creamy and easily able to stand up as a flavour in its own right.

That's where the inspiration for this muffin came from. You've got to use good, full-fat natural yoghurt for it to come through, with the icing really compounding the flavour. You can also make chocolatey yoghurt muffins by adding a couple of teaspoons of cocoa to both icing and muffins.

These muffins always end up gloriously light and crumbly.

*100g caster sugar*
*a pinch of salt*
*1 egg*
*225g full-fat natural*
*   Greek yoghurt*
*100g sunflower oil*
*250g plain flour*
*1 teaspoon baking powder*
*1 teaspoon bicarbonate of soda*

*For the icing*
*200g full-fat natural*
*   Greek yoghurt*
*a heaped tablespoon of*
*   cream cheese*
*plenty of icing sugar*
*   (200–400g), to your taste*

1. Preheat your oven to 190°C /170°C fan/Gas 5. Grease a 12-hole muffin tin with plenty of butter or oil, or line your tins with muffin cases.

2. Into a large bowl, weigh the sugar, salt, egg, yoghurt and oil. Whisk these all together until combined.

3. Dump the flour on top, followed by the baking powder and bicarb, mixing the raising agents into the flour lightly with your fingers to distribute. Then, using a rigid spoon, mix everything together until lumpy but no flour is visible.

4. Spoon your mix into your tin – if any flour becomes visible, just lightly mix it in. Bake for 20–30 minutes, depending on the size of the muffins. Check them regularly and turn down the heat if they're baking too fast. Once the muffins are done, they'll be very springy to the touch. Take them out and leave to cool whilst you make the icing.

5. Scoop your yoghurt and cream cheese into a bowl and add the icing sugar a little at a time, whisking then tasting after each addition. Once you're happy with the taste, give the icing a good whisk and it should puff up and thicken like double cream. Spread this on when the muffins are cool and eat within a day.

# SPICED PARSNIP, PEAR & PECAN MUFFINS

MAKES 6 SUPER MUFFINS, OR 12 SMALLER ONES

This muffin recipe combines a classic flavour combination and some immense alliteration to give a muffin that cannot be bested for moistness. You could go for just parsnips or just pears or just spice – all will give excellent muffins. But this combo is better than the sum of its parts.

Although this recipe finishes up gloriously moist, it is quite heavy when going into the oven. I have therefore reduced the oven temperature and increased the cooking time as the heat will take a little longer to penetrate.

*100g caster sugar*
*a pinch of salt*
*1 egg*
*200g milk*
*100g sunflower oil*
*250g plain flour*
*1½ level teaspoons baking powder*

*½ teaspoon bicarbonate of soda*
*2 teaspoons ground mixed spice*
*2 parsnips, peeled and coarsely grated (about 300g)*
*1 pear, peeled and chopped finely*
*100g pecans, chopped*

1. Preheat your oven to 180°C/160°C fan/Gas 4. Grease a 6- or 12-hole muffin tin with plenty of butter or oil, or line your tin with muffin cases.

2. In a large bowl, mix the sugar, salt, egg, milk and sunflower oil together with a whisk until combined.

4. Add the flour on top, followed by the baking powder, bicarb and mixed spice. Mix the raising agents and spice into your flour with your fingertips to distribute, then use a rigid spoon to fold all your dry ingredients into your wet. The mixture should be lumpy.

5. Add the parsnips and pears and fold these in gently, before spooning the mix into your prepared muffin cases or tin. Sprinkle the chopped pecans on top.

6. Bake for 30–40 minutes for big muffins, but reduce the time for smaller ones. Check them regularly. They'll be springy to the touch when done. Leave them to cool in the tin for at least half an hour.

# LEMON, EXTRA-VIRGIN & POPPY SEED MUFFINS

**MAKES 12 MEDIUM MUFFINS**

The ideal accompaniment to afternoon tea. Not savoury and not overly sweet. And a bit intellectual too, what with the savvy juxtaposition of conflicting flavours combined with the near ubiquitous 'lemon and poppy seed' muffin-meme. If you're not keen on the extra-virgin olive oil idea and just want a solid muffin recipe, I won't be offended. That's the beauty of muffins: you can chop and change and things still work out – all you need to do is replace the extra-virgin with sunflower oil and add a touch more sugar, if desired.

You might want to take that concept and thus this recipe even further. Just think – if lemon works, why not orange? But maybe that won't work with the poppy seeds, so will I try ... chopped hazelnuts? Maybe chuck a few raspberries in there for good measure ...

*200g milk*
*100g caster sugar*
*100g extra-virgin olive oil*
*1 medium egg*
*a pinch of salt*
*grated zest of 1 unwaxed lemon*
*250g self-raising flour*
*50g poppy seeds*

*For the drizzle*
*100g caster sugar*
*juice of 1 lemon*

1. Preheat your oven to 190°C/170°C fan/Gas 5. Grease a muffin tin with plenty of butter or oil, or line your tin with muffin cases.

2. Into a large bowl, weigh the milk, sugar, oil, egg, salt and lemon zest. Whisk together to combine.

3. Dump your flour and poppy seeds onto this liquid mix. Using a wooden or metal spoon, very gently fold everything together until combined. Try not to overwork.

4. Use two spoons to spoon the mix into your tin. Bake for 20–25 minutes, or until the muffins are a medium golden brown. Leave to cool in the tin whilst making the drizzle.

5. Place the lemon juice in a pan and add the caster sugar before placing over a high heat and bringing to the boil. As soon as it's bubbling furiously, remove from the heat.

6. Drizzle the muffins generously with the lemon syrup. Leave to cool, then remove from the tin and enjoy for up to 2 days or freeze.

# MINCEMEAT MUFFINS

MAKES 12 LARGE MUFFINS

I had to include this cheeky extra treat. These muffins are hilariously difficult to ruin and are an amazing way to use up leftover jars of mincemeat at any time of the year.

You could make these at Christmas for an alternative to the endless mince pies. I can even imagine this recipe as a somewhat fashionable alternative to Christmas cake, if you haven't the time, patience or inclination to make a full-blown iced cake. Kind of bare and minimalist. That's a legitimate excuse, right?

*50g caster sugar*
*a pinch of salt*
*1 egg*
*200g full-fat milk*
*100g sunflower oil*
*400g jar mincemeat*

*a handful of extra raisins*
*250g plain flour*
*2 teaspoons baking powder*
*½ teaspoon bicarbonate soda*
*1 teaspoon cinnamon*
*icing sugar, for dusting, optional*

1. Preheat your oven to 190°C/170°C fan/Gas 5. Grease a 12-hole muffin tins with plenty of butter or oil, or line your tins with muffin cases.

2. Into a bowl, weigh the sugar, salt, egg, milk, oil, mincemeat and raisins. Mix together to combine.

3. Add the flour, baking powder, bicarb and cinnamon on top. Mix the raising agents into the dry ingredients with your fingers to distribute evenly. Then fold the mixture together until lumpy but with no flour visible.

4. Scoop into your cases or tins and bake for 30–35 minutes or so, until golden brown and springy when pressed. Leave to cool before serving, then dust lightly with icing sugar. Or not, if you like.

# SQUIDGY GINGERBREAD MUFFINS

MAKES 12 LARGE MUFFINS

This is a recipe I've used for years for a soft, squidgy gingerbread that I usually top with lemon icing. The thing I didn't really notice about it until now is that it's actually just a muffin recipe. The only difference is that you've got to heat a few ingredients in a pan before baking. Therefore, why not reunite it with its muffin family?

And like muffins, this recipe can be chopped and changed. The syrups and sugars can be swapped for different types and the ginger removed entirely, if you like.

This recipe is super-popular with everyone who tries it. I cannot recommend it enough. However: do not use this recipe to make building blocks for the walls of a gingerbread barn. It doesn't work. *(Pictured on page 97.)*

250g golden syrup
150g black treacle
125g dark brown sugar
150g unsalted butter
1-inch piece of fresh
   ginger, finely grated
1 teaspoon ground ginger
250g whole milk
2 medium eggs

1 heaped teaspoon bicarbonate
   of soda
300g plain flour, sieved if
   possible

**For the lemon glaze**
juice of 1 lemon
200g icing sugar

1. Preheat your oven to 170°C/150°C fan/Gas 3. Line two 6-hole muffin tins with large muffin cases.

2. Into a saucepan, weigh the golden syrup, treacle, sugar, butter, grated ginger and ground ginger. Then weigh the milk and eggs. into a small bowl. Place the saucepan over a high heat to melt the butter and sugar and soften the syrups. Use a whisk to make sure everything's combined.

3. Remove from the heat and add the milk and eggs immediately, whisking as soon as they're in so as not to scramble the eggs.

4. Add the bicarbonate and whisk like crazy to distribute. Finally, add the flour and, again, whisk as vigorously as you can, otherwise you end up with a lumpy mix, which isn't good here.

5. Pour your mix straight into your muffin cases and bake for a good 30 minutes at least. These should rise stupendously in the oven, so don't overfill. Leave them to cool in the tin whilst you make the glaze.

6. Put the lemon juice into a pan and then place over a medium heat. Once it's bubbling, remove from the heat and mix in the icing sugar. Brush or pour the glaze over the top of the muffins immediately.

TORTE

# TORTE

The definitions of 'torte' are diverse. For the purposes of this book, I'm going to hijack the word to describe a cake made using little or no wheat flour and ground nuts in its place. It doesn't have to refer to layered slivers filled with ganache, buttercream and all things nice, though it can. It definitely doesn't ever refer to anything that is encapsulated in pastry; see the Sweet chapter on the glorious tart for those (pages 167–184). Tortes can be made in an identical way to cakes, though the lack of flour causes structural insecurity. Without wonderful gluten to hold everything together, tortes have a habit of refusing to rise, of collapsing if they do rise, and of gushing into steaming clumps on your kitchen floor when you try and take them out of the tin – if you manage to get that far.

But after reading the following tips, I'm hopeful you won't encounter any of these issues. The inherent volatility of the torte does lend itself to one overriding, redeeming feature: texture. The torte will never have the sponginess or breadiness that a cake can suffer from.

## THE IDEAL TORTE

The layers of a torte can be thick or thin, though not so thick as to necessitate a long baking time, resulting in a noticeable crust. Presentation can vary from rustic to elaborate: it can be entirely uniced and undecorated if it can stand on its own; or you can spend a huge amount of time crafting the most intricate creation you can imagine, if that's the sort of thing you enjoy.

The colour will vary depending on the ingredients. The top should be a shallow dome. It should not sink in the middle and equally should not peak or split.

On slicing, it should allude to its texture. It should not be tough. On tasting, it should be that perfect balance between crumbly and moist, with enough of a cake-like aspect to hold it together. The flavour of the nuts should never be swamped and should always be considered when choosing additional flavours and ingredients.

## BASIC TORTE RECIPE
### MAKES ONE 9-INCH TORTE

*3 medium eggs*
*140g caster sugar*
*180g ground almonds (or any ground nuts of your choice)*
*a wee pinch of salt*
*flaked nuts, for decorating*

**LINE**

Line the bottom of a 9-inch springform cake tin with baking paper. Grease the sides heavily with butter.

**SEPARATE**

Separate the eggs. Crack an egg forcefully on the side of a large, clean bowl and split the shell in half, catching the yolk in one half and letting the whites drain into the bowl below. Pass the yolk from side to side until there is minimal white left. If the yolk bursts, don't worry. Place the main yolk into another large bowl and scoop any wee bits of yolk out of your whites.

**WHITES**

Whisk your egg whites until stiff. Then, once they're as big as they're going to get, add two tablespoons of sugar and whisk for another few minutes until glossy and smooth.

**WHY**

Greasing and lining your tin is especially important with tortes – they stick like velcro and never come away in one piece if they do stick.

**WHY**

Without creaming butter and sugar to create air, we rely on the rise created by the egg whites. For egg whites to whip up properly, there must not be any yolk present. This is because the fat in the yolk binds to the proteins in the white, stopping them from uncoiling on beating, and from binding to each other to form a great meringue network.

**WHY**

By whisking, you're flattening out the coiled chains of proteins in the whites. Once they're flat, they form a film into which air is beaten. Adding sugar stabilises the mixture – it binds with the proteins and means they can absorb more water, making them strong and elastic.

**YOLKS**

Whisk the egg yolks and the remaining sugar until at least doubled in size and significantly lighter in colour.

**COMBINE**

Add the almonds and salt to the egg yolks and fold them together slowly.

**FOLD**

Add about a third of the whites to the yolks and mix to combine. Then add the rest and fold them in very gently with a metal spoon. Finally, transfer to your lined tin and scatter with flaked or whole nuts.

**WHY**

You can create bubbles by whisking egg yolks as well as egg whites. The mechanical trauma of the sugar rips holes in the yolks, just as it does in butter. Then the fats 'coalesce' (come together) into chains and clusters, held strong with the proteins to give structure to the bubbles.

**WHY**

Fold slowly and gently so as not to force the air out of the yolks. However, you must make sure the mixture is combined completely; clumps of salt are not tasty.

**WHY**

Adding the whites in two stages stabilises the mixture and allows you to mix in the final two-thirds with relative ease. Thus your final fold can be gentle, conserving all that lovely air.

## THE BAKE

For a torte, the intention of baking is to cause the proteins in the eggs to set, as there is no flour to cook. Think of it like a really sugary omelette with ground nuts through it (though don't tell anyone that's what it is – it can ruin the magic a bit). Tortes should be baked straight after the final fold is complete, as the eggs don't hold their structure for long.

The oven should be preheated to 170°C/150°C fan/Gas 3 – just below the temperature you would use for cakes, as you want a gradual rise with a shallow dome. The above mixture, a single layer torte in a 9-inch tin, will take about 20–25 minutes.

If you are baking your torte in lots of thin layers, make sure your tins are properly lined with baking paper. Crank your oven up high (200°C/180°C fan/Gas 6) and bake each layer for about 10 minutes, checking regularly.

Bake until a light golden brown and a skewer comes out clean – you can cover any skewer sins with a dust of icing sugar once cooled.

## VARIATIONS

**BUTTER**  You can make a torte in the same way as you'd make a standard cake, by creaming butter and sugar to create air. If you match your quantity of sugar with butter, you'll have a richer, lighter torte.

**CHOCOLATE**  Melt 150g each of dark chocolate and butter together in the microwave or over a pan of simmering water, and add to the whisked egg yolks and sugar mixture. This is the variation I use on a regular basis and is quite like making a brownie.

**ZEST**  As a matter of course, I tend to incorporate lemon, orange or lime zest into all my tortes. I just add it with the sugar to the egg yolks. You can also make a syrup with the juice and drizzle it over at the end.

**VEG**  Add coarsely grated vegetables to a torte for moistness in the same way you would add them to a cake. Always keep in mind your other ingredients – carrot goes with pecan, courgette goes with pistachio, and beetroot goes with chocolate.

**FRUIT**  I would avoid adding juiced or pulped fruit directly into torte mixes, as this will make it stodgy. Instead, add the zests of citrus fruits, make syrups from fruit juices for drizzling, or add fruit as an accessory on top, raw or stewed.

**EXTRACTS AND ESSENCES**  A teaspoon of almond extract obviously works well in an almond torte, and chocolate extract likewise in a chocolate torte. Vanilla tends to make everything better.

## SUBSTITUTIONS

**NUTS**  The almonds can be replaced with pretty much any nut, ground in a food processor. Try not to grind them for too long, however, as they'll eventually just turn into nut butter.

**SUGAR**  It may seem daft, but you can make a savoury torte. Just mix 3 eggs and 300g ricotta and pour over a tin lined with tomato, feta and herbs to make an upside-down-cake-style dish.

## STORAGE

Tortes freeze beautifully, far better, even, than cake. Once baked and cooled, wrap them in cling film and freeze. You can freeze in the tin until solid if you are worried about them breaking apart in the freezer. Defrost slowly and do not reheat. Tortes will also last for several days at room temperature without going stale (a couple more in the fridge – allow to come back to room temperature before enjoying). Tortes containing butter will stay moist for longer.

## TROUBLESHOOTING

*Why has my torte sunk in the middle?* This can be due to insufficient dry ingredients (some nuts or seeds may require their quantities tweaking), too low an oven temperature, or the eggs being too large (make sure you use medium eggs).

*Why is my torte eggy?* The eggs were too big. Use medium eggs: the weight of the egg (no shell) should be 45–50g.

*Why is my torte dry?* Two things cause dryness: baking for too long or adding too many dry ingredients.

*Why is my torte gooey/stodgy?* It could be underbaked, but it's worth looking at your measuring; too much sugar or butter can cause a really stodgy mix. Equally, if you've overground or overmixed your nuts, this can release their oils, causing stodginess and occasionally collapse.

*Why does my torte have a crust?* It's overbaked. If it has a crust and has only just baked in the middle, you need to drop your oven temperature by 20°C or so, or go for a flatter, wider tin.

*Why has my torte stuck?* Always use non-stick baking paper and heavily grease any areas of bare tin with butter.

*Why hasn't my torte risen?* Don't worry. Even if you've beaten the eggs to maximum fluffiness, your torte won't rise too much. If it's dense, check you've weighed everything correctly or readjust your quantities to suit.

# CHOCOLATE & PASSION FRUIT TORTE
## WITH PASSION FRUIT TRUFFLES
### MAKES ONE 9-INCH TORTE

I'm especially proud of this dessert. It was actually the first recipe of mine ever to be published. You can find it in the *Great British Bake Off* book that year. However far away the final version might have been from what I actually made. And however little I was credited (not at all). And however much money I made (none at all).

But I'm not bitter, and neither is this torte, despite the vast amount of dark chocolate involved. Chocolate and passion fruit is one of those undeniably amazing and for-once-not-so-weird flavour pairings that's omnipresent in posh patisseries. I first discovered it in ice-cream form: try ordering a double cone with a scoop of passion fruit and scoop of chocolate then sit down by yourself and take a moment. *(Pictured overleaf.)*

160g hazelnuts
250g butter
250g good dark chocolate
3 passion fruits
200g caster sugar
6 medium eggs, separated
cocoa powder, for dusting

**For the ganache**
6 passion fruits
300ml double cream
300g dark chocolate (70–75%)

1. Preheat your oven to 170°C/150°C fan/Gas 3. Line the bottom of a 9-inch tin with a sheet of baking paper and grease the sides well.

2. In a food processor, blend about three-quarters of the hazelnuts until finely ground (the consistency of ground almonds), then add the rest of the nuts and pulse until these are roughly chopped. Remove from the processor and set aside.

3. Melt the butter, chocolate and the strained juice from your 3 passion fruits slowly in the microwave or in a bowl over a pan of simmering water.

4. Whilst they are melting, prepare two bowls. In the first bowl, whisk the egg whites with half of the sugar to stiff peaks. In the second, whisk the egg yolks with half of the sugar until lightly coloured.

5. Once the chocolatey mix is melted, fold it into the egg yolks followed by the hazelnuts. Finally, fold in your egg whites as gently as possible. Bake for 45–50 minutes, or until coming away from the sides and a skewer comes out clean. Leave it to cool in the tin before you make the ganache – this should ideally be added to a completely cooled cake.

6. For the ganache, scoop out the insides of the passion fruit into a saucepan. Add the cream and place over a medium heat to bring to the boil. Whilst that's heating, break your chocolate into small chunks and place in a bowl. Once your cream is boiling, pour it through a sieve onto your chocolate, forcing any clinging bits of passion fruit through with a spoon. Mix to amalgamate.

7. Leave the ganache to cool slightly. Remove the cake from the tin and carefully pour over about three-quarters of the ganache to coat the cake. Alternatively, you can spread on the ganache once cooled – the finish doesn't matter if you're going to dust with cocoa, as I do.

8. To make the truffles, chill the rest of the ganache completely. Once cooled, use a teaspoon to scoop out a little of the set mixture and then roll into a sphere using hands dusted with cocoa. Set these on your torte to denote slices. Finally, dust the whole torte with cocoa to finish. I don't, but you might also want to decorate around the edge of the cake with some fresh passion fruit to allude to the otherwise concealed flavour. Your call.

# GRAPEFRUIT POLENTA TORTE
## MAKES AN 8-INCH TORTE

Like those vegan, chicken-esque cubes, my problem with a lot of gluten-free recipes is that they make concessions; they are pretending. But this is no compromise. The heavenly, crumbly texture of this torte is better unbound from the intermolecular shackle that is gluten.

Though the torte does not sacrifice flavour, the method of making it is certainly a compromise between the torte and the cake. I'm using the traditional creaming method, but saving the egg whites to fold in at the end. For a light and crumbly cake it is imperative to do this gently, then treat it as you would a newborn child until it's properly baked. No peeking in the oven. *(Pictured overleaf.)*

*150g softened, salted butter*
*150g caster sugar*
*finely grated zest of*
*    1 large ruby grapefruit*
*3 medium eggs, separated*
*150g fine polenta*
*170g ground almonds*
*2 teaspoons gluten-free*
*    baking powder*

*For the candied grapefruit*
*1 whole ruby grapefruit*
*100g caster sugar*
*200g water*

*For the drizzle*
*100g caster sugar*
*juice of 1 ruby grapefruit*
*    (from the zested fruit above)*

1. Preheat your oven to 160°C/140°C/Gas 3. Line the bottom of an 8-inch springform tin (or high-sided 7-inch cake tin) with a sheet of baking paper and grease the sides well.

2. In a large bowl, beat the butter, sugar and zest together with an electric mixer or wooden spoon. Keep going until the mix is white and mousse-like (the softer the butter, the quicker this will happen).

3. Add the yolks, one at a time, beating well after each addition.

4. In a separate bowl, whisk the egg whites until light and fluffy.

5. Once the egg yolks are mixed in, add the polenta, almonds and baking powder. Fold these in gently with a large spoon until completely combined, then add a third of the egg whites and mix these in too. Finally, fold in the last of the whites and scoop the mix into your lined and greased tin.

6. Transfer to the middle shelf of your oven and bake for 30–35 minutes, or until a light golden brown. It should spring back when pressed and a skewer should come out clean. Leave it in the tin to cool gradually.

7. Whilst it's baking, make the candied ruby grapefruit. Slice your fruit any way you like whilst you heat the sugar and water together in a pan. Bring the sugary mix to a boil, then add the grapefruit slices before boiling for 5 minutes. After this time, turn the fruit over and reduce the heat to a gentle simmer. You want to reduce it to a thick syrup and to cook your grapefruit until the skins are translucent. This will take about 20 minutes.

8. To finish, make a drizzle by bringing the sugar and the juice from your zested grapefruit to a boil in a pan. As soon as it's bubbling furiously, remove from the heat. Use a knife or skewer to poke loads of holes in your still-warm cake, then drizzle your syrup all over so that it soaks in easily. Finally, decorate with your candied fruit.

OPPOSITE: GRAPEFRUIT POLENTA TORTE

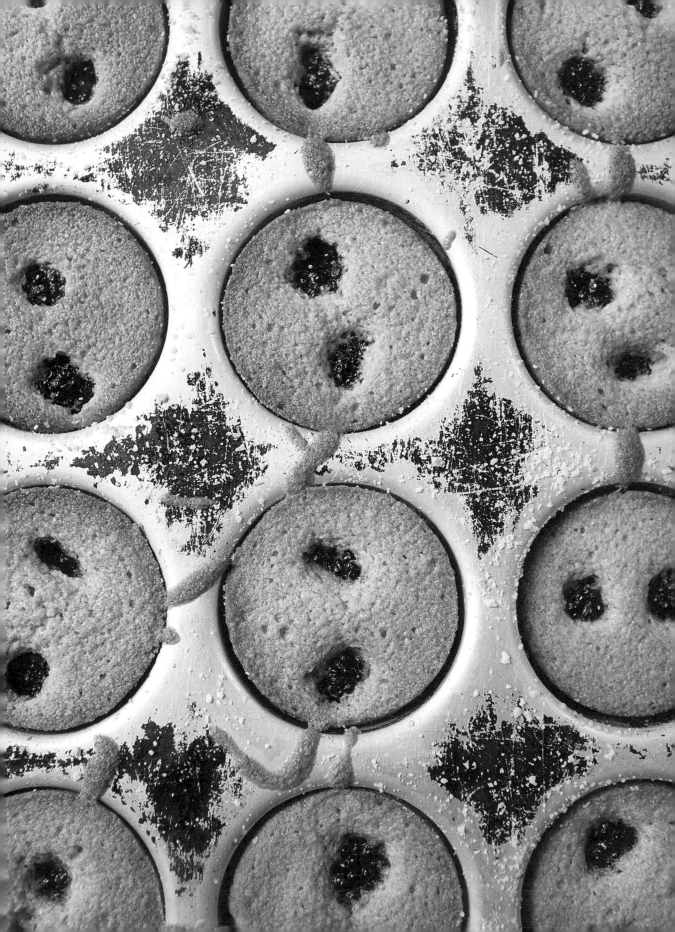

# FRIANDS

MAKES 12 MUFFIN-SIZED FRIANDS

Though not really what you'd think of when you hear the word 'torte', friands fit best into this chapter. They're so easy to make and so very moist and delicious that I couldn't leave them out. They are made with the same mix as financiers.

They get their primary flavour from the 'beurre noisette': melted then browned butter. This is why my recipe contains more butter than most. You can reduce this to your taste if you like, but combined with the toasted ground nuts, you get a really nutty-tasting recipe.

Topping with peach works well (it kind of sinks in a bit), as do all manner of other soft fruit and berries, chocolate and more nuts. Indeed, you don't even need to use almonds – you can use any nut you like.

*80g ground almonds*
*125g salted butter*
*150g icing sugar*
*50g plain flour*

*3 egg whites*
*soft fruit or berries, optional*
*icing sugar, for dusting*

1. Preheat your oven to 180°C/160°C fan/Gas 4. Grease any wee tins – I'd go for little ramekins if you have them – but beware that you need to be able to get your cakes out afterwards, so nothing too awkward.

2. Scatter the ground almonds over a baking tray and place them on the top shelf in the oven. This is just to lightly toast them and contribute to the flavour of the final cake; 5 minutes will do.

3. Melt the butter in a pan over a high heat. Once it has melted, keep cooking until you've nearly burnt it – it should go a nice dark brown colour. Then remove from the heat and leave to cool.

4. In a large bowl, mix your icing sugar, flour, toasted almonds and egg whites together, mixing vigorously to combine. Then drizzle in the butter, stirring all the time, until the mixture is amalgamated.

5. Spoon the mixture into your tins – you want them just over a centimetre deep. Top with fruit, if using, then bake for 10–12 minutes until just golden. Leave to cool, then dust with icing sugar to serve.

# TORTA CAPRESE

MAKES ONE 9-INCH TORTE

I must give credit where credit is due and admit that this is my sister's recipe. I demanded it from her for this book and she agreed, reluctantly. She used to type up all her recipes and keep them in a neat plastic folder. This was in stark contrast to me – I'd keep track of my favourite recipes by looking for the stuck-together pages in the family cookbooks.

This is a funny one because it's not made like most tortes or cakes, though the ingredients are of fairly similar proportion. It's very simple, very rich and very modifiable, and a good base from which to experiment.

200g butter
200g good dark chocolate
150g caster sugar
4 medium eggs
1 heaped tablespoon of
    cocoa powder

250g ground almonds
fresh raspberries, to serve
crème fraîche, to serve

1. Preheat your oven to 170°C/150°C/Gas 3. Line the bottom of a 9-inch springform cake tin with baking paper and grease the sides well.

2. First, melt the butter in a pan or in the microwave and set aside to cool.

3. In a food processor, blitz the chocolate until pretty much ground up but with a few wee lumps left.

4. Into a large bowl, weigh the sugar and eggs into a large bowl and whisk with an electric mixer on the highest speed for a good 10 minutes. It should be extremely light and fluffy.

5. Add the cocoa powder, almonds and blitzed chocolate and fold these in as gently as you can, so as to preserve the air you've whipped up. Then add the melted butter and fold everything together.

6. Bake for approximately 45 minutes, or until firm and bouncy. Check after 30 minutes and if it is browning too fast, turn the oven down by at least 10°C. Leave to cool in the tin, then serve cold with raspberries and crème fraîche.

# PISTACHIO, LIME & COURGETTE TORTE

MAKES ONE 7-INCH TORTE

I'm not entirely sure where the idea for this awesome combination came from, but I have a feeling an anaesthetist recommended it or one similar to it whilst I was shadowing her in theatre for a day. I'm pretty sure it was an anaesthetist anyway. It definitely wasn't a surgeon; they're not such good bakers, as a rule. It's amazing how fancy you can make something look by adding loads of layers. Normally I'd say pretentious, but when curd's involved I'm of the belief that layers correlate positively with pleasure.

180g pistachios (ground in a
    food processor)
1 medium courgette
3 medium eggs, separated
finely grated zest of 1 lime,
    plus extra for decoration
140g caster sugar
1 x quantity lime curd
    (see page 36)

icing sugar, for dusting

**For the lime drizzle**
juice of 1 lime
    (from the zested fruit above)
50g caster sugar

1. Preheat the oven to 170°C/150°C fan/Gas 3. Line the bottom of two 7-inch cake tins with baking paper and grease the sides well.

2. Peel the courgette, then grate it coarsely. Wrap this in kitchen paper to soak up the excess moisture then set aside.

3. To the yolks, add the lime zest and half your sugar. Whisk vigorously until lighter in colour and noticeably expanded. Then whisk the egg whites to stiff peaks, adding the rest of the sugar to stabilise them.

4. Fold the ground pistachios into the yolks, followed by the courgettes and finally the egg whites. Divide this mix between your two cake tins and bake for 20–25 minutes or until risen and springy. Leave to cool in the tins.

5. Whilst they're cooling, make the drizzle by heating the lime juice and sugar in a pan until the mixture is boiling. Then remove it from the heat.

6. Cut each cake in half horizontally, to give four layers of cake. Brush the drizzle conservatively on the crumb-side of all the cakes before leaving them to cool completely whilst you make the curd (see page 36).

7. To assemble, place a layer of cake onto a serving plate, spread a layer of lime curd over it and then sandwich another layer of cake on top. Repeat until you've no more cake left. Top with a few shavings of lime zest and an inevitable dusting of icing sugar.

BISCUIT

# BISCUIT

The biscuit is a flat, brittle cake. Its primary ingredients are sugar, flour and fat, and it can be crisp, crumbly or chewy with legitimacy. It can contain added liquid, nuts, chunks and flavouring, but not so much as to affect the shape and structural integrity. As far as this book goes, a biscuit is not a cookie (as in the US-style); the 'cookie' is a subsection of biscuits composed of chewy, egg-containing recipes.

The biscuit is the easiest style of baking to pull off but the hardest to master. Small modifications make large differences. I believe that it is best to start at the beginning with the simplest biscuit: shortbread. The techniques used in this humble three-ingredient culinary *chef d'oeuvre* are then only marginally modified for every biscuit recipe in the world.

The key to a crumbly biscuit is to work the dough as little as possible after adding the flour. There is a reasonable amount of water in butter and plenty to cause ample gluten formation. Then you can chill your biscuit dough to help the biscuits hold their shape when it's time to bake. And it's the bake that's quite hard to judge, for biscuits are still soft when they're done. It will take a few attempts to get it perfect.

## THE IDEAL BISCUIT

A biscuit can be any shape you like, but if cut as round, they should all be round; if cut as squares, they should all be square. They should not spread excessively in the oven. Consistency is held in high regard and so uniformity is preferred; it prevents fights, at least. Each should only be large enough to serve one person, unless in premeditated circumstances.

The colour will depend on the bake. A shortbread should be pale without any hint of brown, but still crumble easily. A cookie should be darker with obvious cracks, and should snap or bend depending on your preference. They should never be burnt. The taste will depend on your aim, but it should at least be appropriate to style. For example, a shortbread biscuit should never, ever have any bitterness or caramel-style notes. This is a sign of overbaking. Equally, a cookie shouldn't be cloying or crumbly, and the taste of toasted sugar should dominate any buttery richness.

## BASIC SHORTBREAD BISCUIT RECIPE

*200g softened, salted butter*
*100g caster sugar*
*300g plain flour*
*caster sugar, for sprinkling*

### LINE

Line a large, flat baking tray with baking paper. You can use the odd dot of butter to stick it down.

### SMOOSH

Into a large bowl, weigh the butter and sugar. If your butter isn't soft, zap it in the microwave on low power until squishy. Using a rigid spoon, mix these together until they are combined and smooth. The mixture should *not* become light and fluffy.

### COMBINE

Add the flour and combine, first with the spoon and then with your hands if it becomes difficult to work. You should be as gentle as possible when doing this. There should be no flour visible in your final dough. You can then chill your dough in the fridge for up to several days to improve the final texture.

### WHY

Stuck biscuits are a disaster. And biscuits are liable to stick due to their minimal gluten formation; the remaining starch and protein is free to flop out and stick to anything it can.

### WHY

This step is not like creaming in cake-making. You're just looking to combine the ingredients, dissolving the sugar in the butter to an extent. You do not want to beat in loads of air; this will cause a cracking, expanding, spongy biscuit.

### WHY

Kneading is good in bread-making because it develops the gluten to give a nice chewy, bubbly texture. It is bad in almost every other aspect of baking, especially in cakes and biscuits. If you remember that, then you're set to be a good baker. Try to work the biscuit dough as little as possible if you want a crumbly, melt-in-the-mouth texture.

### CUT

Flatten your dough by dusting it with flour (or placing it between two flat sheets of cling film) then rolling out, or just pressing down with your hand to the thickness you are after. Then cut out the shapes you would like and place on your prepared tray, dusting with caster sugar if desired.

### CHILL

Place your biscuits in the fridge for at least 15–20 minutes, or up to a day.

### WHY

Roll out the dough to the thickness you want your final biscuits to be, as they will not expand much in the oven. You should have incorporated minimal air and you've added no raising agent. The exception to this rule is in cookie-making – in this case, you can expect your biscuits to pancake and bloom slightly.

### WHY

This is a step that is often forgotten in biscuit-making, but seems to be an essential in pastry-making. The truth: biscuits and pastry are pretty similar, and the same rules apply. If you rest them in the fridge, you'll firm up the butter so they don't flatten out in the oven, and you'll allow the gluten matrix to relax for a more crumbly final texture.

## THE BAKE

The bake in biscuits is the most essential part, so set timers and don't get distracted. You can open the oven to check as often as you like; there's no flimsy structure to disrupt here.

For a shortbread-style recipe, you want very little colour but a proper crisp bake. This calls for a low oven temperature: 160°C/140°C fan/Gas 3. It also means that if you do forget about the biscuits for five minutes or so, you won't notice much difference. Baking time will depend heavily on the thickness of biscuit that you go for: I'd say about 10 minutes for super-thin discs; 20 minutes for finger-thickness shortbread; and add on 5 minutes for every couple of millimetres. The key is to check regularly and if any are beginning to brown at the edges, take out the tray.

For snappy or chewy biscuits, bake at a higher temperature. This allows the outer surface to dry out quickly and then become caramelised with toffee-esque flavours. If you would like the inside of the biscuit to remain soft, this stage can be reached in only 10 minutes. If you would prefer completely snappy biscuits, bake for longer. High temperature baking is inappropriate in short biscuits because it leads to an almost bitter taste and a texture that is far too snappy at the expense of crumbliness.

Leave to cool on the tray, or on a cooling rack if you prefer.

## VARIATIONS

**COOKIES** To make awesome cookies, simply add 2 medium eggs and a teaspoon of bicarb to the basic recipe, before you add the flour. It's best to chill your dough after mixing and before baking. They will spread out in the oven, so there's no need to roll them out like shortbread – just cut your dough into lumps and squish onto your baking sheet.

**OATS** Oats should only ever be added to cookies. You should leave out half to two-thirds of the flour, and replace this quantity with whole rolled oats. You cannot replace all the flour with oats.

**CHOPPED NUTS/CHOCOLATE CHIPS/FRUIT** Whatever your recipe, my rule on adding nuts, chocolate chips or dried fruit is the same: go for 'a couple of handfuls' or, if in doubt, 'a small packet'. You don't need to change the recipe for these, though if adding ground nuts, reduce the flour a touch (at least half the quantity of nuts added). The zest of fruit can also add further complexity.

**SNAPPY** If you want a useable dough for things like custard creams, empire biscuits or jammy dodgers, I'd use shortbread. Add an egg yolk to your recipe with the butter and sugar and bake 20°C higher for a few minutes' less. This will make your biscuits snappy, as opposed to crumbly.

**SPICES** Spices in biscuits should dominate the flavour profile completely. So for an awesome gingerbread, for example, just add an egg (for snappiness), a teaspoon of bicarb and 3 teaspoons of ground ginger with the flour to my basic shortbread recipe. Any spice or herb can and should be used – please experiment.

**ICING**   Mix icing sugar with a few tablespoons of boiling water until gooey, then spread on top when your biscuits are cooled. If you're a purist, you can make your own royal icing (super-hard icing) by whisking together an egg white, 400g icing sugar and the juice of half a lemon.

**EXTRACTS**   Most extracts work well in biscuits, especially vanilla, orange blossom water, almond, rosewater and aroma panettone. Add them at the start.

**CHOCOLATE**   Who doesn't like chocolate biscuits? You can dip any finished biscuit in chocolate for favourable results. Simply melt some chocolate (see page 28) and dunk the tops or sides of your biscuits in.

**BISCOTTI**   These delicious wee things are baked twice: once in a long sausage, then they're sliced up and baked again individually on both sides. These are a bit more specialist, so use the Seedy Biscotti recipe on page 144 as a guide. The reason I include them here is to demonstrate the similarities to their baking cousins: all you're doing is substituting the butter for eggs, and adding a little more sugar.

## SUBSTITUTIONS

**FLOUR**   The flour can be replaced with any gluten-free plain flour in all the above variations – however, you should add a little extra to be on the safe side. Gluten-free flour works particularly well in oat cookies.

**EGGS**   Eggs can be replaced with vegan substitutes, or you can use all whites if you want your biscuits a bit healthier. Though bear in mind that biscuits are supposed to be unhealthy.

**SUGAR**   If you don't have caster, any fine sugar can be used – icing sugar will work in the vast majority of biscuits. Don't use granulated or you get a gritty texture. Brown sugars shouldn't be used in shortbreads, but will work in any other biscuit.

**BUTTER**   Butter can be substituted for shortening (hard margarine), but you shouldn't use soft baking spread. Oil can be used in cookies, but they'll end up a bit shiny and flat.

## STORAGE

Once completely cooled, biscuits and cookies should be stored in an airtight container at room temperature and eaten within 3–4 days of baking. However, they will begin to deteriorate within hours, so try to eat them as soon as possible. I maintain that the best time to store your biscuits is pre-baking, for they don't take long in the oven.

Biscuits freeze well, wrapped in cling film or in freezer bags. In fact, if your biscuit is a bit soft for your liking, try eating them straight from frozen; you might be pleasantly surprised by the texture. Otherwise, let them defrost for half an hour or so before enjoying.

# TROUBLESHOOTING

*Why is my shortbread hard and snappy?* The most common reason for a hard biscuit is baking for too long at too high a temperature. If you turn your oven down a little, it gives you leeway if you forget about it. Otherwise, remember not to overwork your dough after adding the flour and make sure all your measurements are correct.

*Why are my biscuits soft, squidgy or pale?* You may not have baked your biscuits for long enough and so they have retained too much moisture. If they're quite dark on top, turn your oven down and bake for longer. You should also check your baking tray – if it's too thick, this can lead to biscuits burnt on the top but soft underneath. Finally, it could be your storage methods – make sure you only store after complete cooling, and that any seals are completely airtight.

*Why are my cookies spreading and flat?* I often encounter this problem from newbie biscuiteers who are otherwise excellent cake-makers. If you overcream your butter and sugar, your biscuits will spread out. Also, make sure you chill your biscuits or dough before baking, as that will prevent them spreading out too much in the oven. Again, incorrect measuring or using a recipe with too much butter will cause spreading, as will a recipe with tons of raising agent.

*Why are my cookies not chewy?* Either you've overcooked them (the most likely option) or you've skimped on the butter. Shame on you. If your definition and my definition of 'chewy' are different, add yet more butter, a touch more sugar and enjoy your delicious stodge.

*Why are the bottoms of my biscuits burned?* Many people would attest that your baking tray is too thin, but it's not. This usually happens when your heating element is on the bottom of the oven, and your biscuits burn from underneath. To solve this, place on a higher shelf and turn the oven down a notch to compensate. If this still doesn't work, place another tray between your tray and the bottom of the oven; this will reflect most of the heat back and leave your biscuits sheltered.

*Why are my biscuits tough?* This is usually a problem with measuring (adding too much flour) but it can also be due to overworking in a hot environment, too. If you develop too much gluten, especially in the presence of egg or liquid, your biscuits will range from leathery to pork crackling.

# HAZELNUT SHORTBREAD

MAKES ABOUT 16 SHORTBREAD FINGERS

This is a simple recipe that, as far as I know, is infallible. You cannot ruin this recipe. Even if you drop it on the floor, it still looks rustic and nonchalant.

If you examine the ingredients, you can see how this recipe works – some might say how all of baking works. The standard shortbread recipe is 3:2:1 – flour:butter:sugar, right? Here I've added hazelnuts, which will be blitzed to a combination of powder and chunks.

These will, to an extent, dry out the biscuit. So I've reduced the flour accordingly. Blitzing also releases some of the oils within the nuts, and so that's why I've scrimped on the butter, too.

This is a simplified way of how I begin to form any recipe, and I think it shows just how logical baking is.

*125g raw hazelnuts*
*175g softened, salted butter*
*100g caster sugar*
*200g plain flour*

1.  Preheat your oven to 180°C/160°C fan/Gas 4. Line a baking tray with a sheet of baking paper. Prepare your hazelnuts by blitzing them in a food processor until you have a combination of roughly ground and chopped nuts.

2.  In a large bowl, cream together the butter and caster sugar using a wooden spoon. You don't need to be too vigorous in your mixing, just enough to combine them.

3.  Using your wooden spoon again, gently mix in the hazelnuts and flour until just incorporated. This mixture will become quite stiff so you may need to use your hands. Try not to mix too much or you'll have tough biscuits.

4.  Using your hands or a scraper, scoop the dough out onto the tray and press it out to fill the lined tray, to the thickness of two £1 coins on top of each other. You could use a biscuit cutter to cut it into shapes before baking, but I like the sheer effect of cutting it after it's baked.

5.  Bake for about 15–20 minutes, or until just blushing golden brown at the edges. Then, as soon as it's out of the oven, cut your biscuits into sharp-edged parallelograms, discarding the edge bits. The middle will be soft to begin with, but will harden up in time.

# CHOCOLATE ORANGE COOKIES

MAKES 12 COOKIES

These cookies are some of the most delicious things you can bake in a hurry – from start to finish, you're talking half an hour, if necessary. Ideally, however, you should make the dough and chill it for up to several days in advance of baking; after that, you'll have the most flavoursome, crumbly textured cookies you can imagine.

Chocolate and orange is a flavour combination that is well known and loved. So these cookies are going to be a hit wherever you go. But what makes these guys special is the balance of flavour. Don't be tempted to use anything but dark chocolate; I've tried this with milk chocolate and it ends up too sickly sweet, at least for my taste.

And please get some orange blossom water. It adds a delicate aroma that goes brilliantly with the sweet dough and the bitter, dark chocolate. I didn't know a cookie could be so complex.

150g softened, salted butter
150g caster sugar
finely grated zest of
    1 large orange
1 large egg
1 teaspoon orange blossom
    water, optional

225g plain flour
½ teaspoon baking powder
200g dark chocolate (chips or
    chopped into chunks)

1. Preheat your oven to 200°C/180°C fan/Gas 6. Line a baking tray with a sheet of baking paper.

2. In a large bowl, beat together the butter, sugar and zest with a wooden spoon until paste-like. Then add the egg and orange blossom water and beat until smooth.

3. Add the flour, baking powder and chocolate chips and stir everything together. Feel free to use your hands if it gets tough, but please don't overwork it and definitely don't knead it. Don't develop that gluten.

4. At this point, you can wrap and chill the dough for up to two days. Otherwise, tear it into 12 roughly equal lumps and position on your baking tray with plenty of space between each one.

5. Bake for 10–15 minutes, or until just light brown at the edges (they'll still be soft in the middle when baked). You can overbake to give them a snappy texture, or deliberately underbake to make them floppy. Neither of these is a bad thing.

# THE ULTIMATE MILLIONAIRE'S SHORTBREAD
MAKES 16 SHORTBREAD SLICES

It's not often that I am arrogant enough to believe that my recipe should be the standard on which all others are based. But here I am saying just that. It's not only the best caramel shortcake I've ever had, but I've gone to great pains to keep the steps and ingredients very simple, too. The keys to perfection are as follows:

- A simple, crumbly shortbread. A standard 3:2:1 shortbread recipe is ideal for this. Don't overbake it.

- Smooth, gooey caramel. Often, people ask me how to make a stodgy caramel as opposed to a hard caramel. The truth? Butter. And lots of it. But I find that doing things the old-fashioned way helps too – using half a tin of condensed milk will stabilise your mixture and avert disaster. Then add more butter.

- The chocolate must be perfectly tempered. Fortunately, my guide on page 28 shows you the cheat's way to perfect melted chocolate. It does require that you start out with a good-quality dark chocolate. Worried about all that butter? Just have a smaller slice and develop some self-control.

*For the shortbread base*
*100g softened, salted butter*
*50g caster sugar*
*150g plain flour*

*For the caramel*
*½ x 200g tin condensed milk*
*150g salted butter*
*50g caster sugar*
*50g golden syrup*

*For the chocolate topping*
*200g dark chocolate*
  *(70–80% cocoa solids)*

1. Preheat your oven to 160°C/140°C fan/Gas 3. Line an 8-inch square brownie tin with baking paper and grease the sides.

2. To make the shortbread, use a wooden spoon to combine the butter with the sugar in a large bowl until it forms a paste. Add the flour and gently mix it all together. Use your hands to work the mix until it mops up all the crumbs – you don't need to add any extra liquid.

3. Press this out flat with your hands so that it fills your lined tin, then bake for 10–15 minutes or until it is just blushing golden brown at the edges. Leave to cool in the tin.

4. Whilst it's baking, start the caramel. Weigh all the ingredients into a saucepan and place on a medium-high heat, stirring gently. Watch it closely as you stir – you should start to see little slivers of brown where it has stuck to the bottom of the pan. If you see these bits, stir them in vigorously and turn the heat down to low-medium. Simmer gently until it is a colour that you like – I go for a deep, golden brown.

5. When ready, pour your dark caramel onto your biscuit base and spread it over the top with a knife. To even out the surface, pick up your tin and drop it onto the countertop with a bang. Leave this to cool for at least an hour (or overnight) before adding the chocolate topping, or the heat will ruin your careful chocolate work.

6. Break about three-quarters of the chocolate into a microwaveable bowl and chop the rest very finely (see page 30). Zap your chunks in a microwave on full power for 15 seconds at a time, stirring in between (or melt over a bowl of simmering water). Once melted, add your finely chopped chocolate and stir until they are combined.

7. Pour it onto your cooled caramel surface and spread gently with a knife. Again, to even the surface, pick it up and drop it onto your countertop, or give it a shake in the tin. If you like, you can lay a sheet of cling film on top of your chocolate for an extra shiny surface, but pull it tight to get rid of the wrinkles. Leave it to set for another hour (NEVER in the fridge), before slicing into squares. Heat your knife with water from the kettle to make slicing easier.

# SEEDY BISCOTTI

MAKES ABOUT 24 BISCOTTI

The dough in this recipe can be used to make biscotti containing any ingredients you like. This particular variation is one I'd recommend trying. It's inspired by the archetypal British seedy cake, which I view as an afternoon tea staple. If you fancy making one, just combine my standard cake mix (see page 42) with 3 heaped teaspoons caraway seeds in a 2lb loaf tin.

I do love seedy cake, but caraway works even better in the crunchy twice-baked brilliance that is biscotti. If you're a true show-off, dip them in chocolate. Chocolate and caraway is another one of those snazzy flavour pairings that's cemented in evidence – it just works.

These can be made in advance and given as a gift. Whilst they may look fancy, it's as simple as mixing everything together.

*300g plain flour, plus extra*
   *for dusting*
*2 teaspoons baking powder*
*3 teaspoons caraway seeds*
*200g caster sugar*

*3 medium eggs*
*finely grated zest of 1 lemon*
*200g shelled pistachios*
*200g dried sour cherries,*
   *chopped*

1. Preheat your oven to 180°C/160°C/Gas 4. Line a large baking tray with a sheet of baking paper.

2. Into a large bowl, weigh the flour, baking powder, caraway seeds and sugar, then mix together to combine. Add the eggs, zest, pistachios and dried cherries, and mix everything together into a dough using a wooden spoon.

3. Turn your dough out onto a floured surface. Dust with more flour and divide the dough into two. Roughly shape each into a long sausage using floured hands – you want them as long as the baking tray. Once shaped, place them on the baking tray, leaving as much space as you can between them as they will expand.

4. First, bake in the oven for about 30 minutes until risen and very slightly golden. Then remove from the oven and reduce the oven temperature to 140°C/120°C fan/Gas 1.

5. Leave your risen sausages to cool for 10 minutes, then cut them into slices about 1cm thick using a bread knife. Lay these slices out flat on your baking tray (you might need two trays). Bake for 15 minutes in your low oven, then turn each slice over and bake for another 15 minutes on the other side. Leave to cool on the tray. (If you're giving these away as a gift, bag or jar them as soon as possible to keep them fresh for up to several weeks.)

# ICED RINGS

These biscuits are my favourite and a good opportunity to show off a basic hybrid biscuit dough. This is definitely not a shortbread, but it isn't a cookie either. If you're not a fan of the crumbly texture of shortbread, you can use this same mix to make jammy dodgers, custard creams or empire biscuits. (That's why you won't find recipes for these in here – I believe it would use up valuable pages that should be saved for other things.)

   I like my iced rings pure and simple, so there's shameless use of flavourless food colouring here. But you can introduce new flavours by incorporating them into your icing: try rosewater, lemon juice or orange blossom water (along with the appropriate pink, yellow or orange food colouring).

*50g caster sugar*
*100g softened, salted butter*
*1 medium egg yolk*
*1 teaspoon vanilla extract*
*150g plain flour,*
   *plus extra for dusting*

*25g cornflour*
*about 200g icing sugar or*
   *royal icing sugar*
   *(for hard icing)*
*food colouring of your choice*

1. Preheat your oven to 180°C/160°C/Gas 4. Line a baking tray with a sheet of baking paper.

2. Into a large bowl, weigh the caster sugar, butter, egg yolk and vanilla. Use a wooden spoon to combine them together into a soft paste, then add the flour and cornflour and bring it all together gently, using your hands if the mix is too stiff. Once made, you can cover and chill your dough for up to several days if you wish.

3. Place your dough on a floured surface, dust with more flour and roll out to the thickness of a £1 coin. Using a large round biscuit cutter, cut out circles, then make them into rings by cutting out the centre using a smaller round cutter. Any leftovers can be smooshed together and rolled out again.

4. Place your rings on the baking tray and bake for 10 minutes or so, until slightly firm to the touch but with little sign of browning. You want them pale. Once done, leave them to cool on the tray.

5. I like to make two icings of different colours and feather them. Place some icing sugar and your food colouring into a bowl. Boil a kettle and pour the water into a jug, before adding a few teaspoons to your icing sugar. Mix everything together. If it doesn't turn into a paste, add another teaspoon of water, then stir again. Keep doing this until it just forms a spreadable goo. You can add more icing sugar to thicken it up if you go too far.

6. To feather, start by dipping the top of a cooled biscuit in your first colour of icing, holding it upside down to let the excess drip off. Then lightly drizzle (or pipe using a 1–2mm hole) some straight lines across your biscuit in your second colour of icing. Draw a toothpick across your biscuits perpendicular to the line of icing, then leave to set before enjoying at tea time.

SHORT

# SHORT

Shortcrust pastry (pâte brisée) is a mixture of flour and butter, with liquid added to bring it together into a dough. It is made without sugar and without lamination (see the Puff chapter, page 201). In short, it is the simplest pastry. Not that it always seems it, with chefs piling on unnecessary additions in a perpetual quest for originality, contributing to the cliché that pastry-making is, somehow, not simple. You don't need to be born with cold hands and there is no knack. Any problem is not in your genetics; it's all in the method.

The number one rule in pastry is *not* to keep everything cold, or work it too much, or any other such banalities. It's all in the addition of the water. Too much is a disaster and you'll end up with a chewy, bready crust; too little makes your pastry beautifully crumbly but impossible to serve or eat.

Shortcrust pastry is not just for savoury dishes – indeed, it is the most adaptable pastry to have in your fridge because it can be used for pretty much anything. An apple pie made with sweet pastry? Are you mad?

## THE IDEAL SHORTCRUST PASTRY

The ideal shortcrust pastry should never be rolled thicker than a £1 coin. Ever. Bearing this in mind, it should have the strength to hold itself together when sliced, despite its thinness. When broken in two, it should come apart with an exquisite combination of 'crumble' and 'snap'. It should almost melt in the mouth, but also have a little bite. It should not be overly dry, and it should not be chewy or crispy.

The taste should be rich and buttery, but not so rich as to prevent copious consumption. It should be baked to a golden brown colour; any darker and it begins to taste burnt. It should never have a soggy bottom, unless you're into that sort of thing.

## BASIC SHORTCRUST PASTRY RECIPE
### MAKES ONE LARGE PASTRY CASE, WITH A LITTLE LEFT OVER FOR A FEW JAM TARTS

*300g plain flour, plus extra for dusting*
*150g chilled, salted butter*
*75g ice-cold water*

### GREASE

Grease your tart tin with lots of butter. Don't use baking paper. Your tin should be loose bottomed and made of metal. If the finished bake is going to be served in the dish, glass is acceptable.

### RUB

Weigh the flour into a large bowl. Cut the butter into manageable chunks and add to the flour. Scoop up some butter and flour in both hands, then rub them into each other. Do this by running your thumbs over your fingers, using your fingers like a washboard. Your thumbs should make little circular motions.

### BREADCRUMBS

Continue to rub until your mixture looks like breadcrumbs. Once you think you're there, give the bowl a shake to bring any lumps of butter to the top, then rub these in.

### HOW

In pastry, the idea is to develop minimal gluten. It therefore has a tendency to stick to the tin, so greasing must be severe. As for your tin choice – ideally go for metal. Ceramic or stone dishes have no place in your baking life; they don't transfer the heat from the oven very well and you'll end up with a soggy bottom.

### HOW

You could use a food processor here, but that has the potential to develop the gluten and cause a tough, chewy pastry. Rubbing by hand also lets you get a feel for the right texture, and saves on the washing up.

### HOW

Any small lumps of butter will cause inconsistencies in the strength of your pastry, making it more likely to fall apart once baked. Butter has no structural integrity; only the flour does.

### WATER

Weigh out the water and add around three-quarters to the bowl. Swirl a knife around to incorporate it before using your hands to see if it comes together.

### DOUGH

Add more water, a little at a time (use the whole lot if needed) and work it in until you've mopped up any free crumbs from the side of the bowl. This might take a little 'almost kneading', but that's fine.

### CHILL

Smoosh your dough flat, wrap it tightly in cling film and chill for as long as you can spare – anything from 15 minutes to 3 days is fine.

### HOW

The quantity of water needed will vary depending on the 'strength' of the flour (flours with more protein will absorb more water) and the water content of both your butter and flour. Better to be on the dry side than the wet side.

### HOW

Yes, gluten development can cause a doughy pastry. But the way to guarantee a doughy pastry is to add too much liquid, so if you're struggling between adding a bit more liquid or kneading it a little to bring it together, always go for the latter.

### WHY

Chilling causes the gluten to relax and so the pastry will be under less tension. This makes it much easier to roll out and the pastry more crumbly. The longer you chill for, the better. You should smoosh it a wee bit at this stage because then the rolling pin has less work to do.

### DUST

Dust a clean, dry surface with flour, add your pastry (or however much of it you want to use) and add more flour on top. Roll out, trying to keep the dough a uniform thickness. After every few rolls, move the pastry around and turn it slightly to make sure it hasn't stuck.

### ROLL

Once the pastry is the thickness of a £1 coin, cut out the appropriate size and place it in your prepared tin. Always leave at least some pastry dangling over the edge of the tin if your pie or tart does not have a lid. This will be trimmed after baking. Prick the base all over with a fork.

### CHILL

Finally, chill your pastry case for 10–15 minutes before baking, if you can.

### WHY

A good pastry may stick or it may fall apart. Feel free to add plenty of flour or patch with bits from the side if this is the case. Flouring your rolling pin can make rolling out much easier.

### WHY

Because of the elasticity of the gluten, pastry has a tendency to shrink when heated. Leaving a little dangling over the edge of the tin adds tension to the pastry to stop it shrinking, and gives you a bit to play with if it does insist on shrinking back. Pricking the base prevents large air pockets forming during the bake causing unsightly bubbles.

### WHY

Again, we want to give the gluten time to relax – it does this best at cold temperatures so put your case in the fridge. This will prevent shrinkage.

## THE BAKE

Blind baking is used for the majority of open pies, tarts and quiches. This is when you bake your pastry case without any filling, so as to avoid the dreaded soggy bottom. To do it, preheat your oven to 180°C/160°C fan/Gas 4. Tear off a large square of baking paper and place it on top of your chilled tart case. Weigh it down with some loose change, preferably coppers – I tend to use whatever's in my pocket. You can use baking beans, but these don't transfer heat as rapidly as metal coins. Bake for 25–30 minutes for a large tart case, or 15–20 minutes for smaller individual cases. Then remove the paper and weight and bake for another 10 minutes to brown and crisp. If a dry filling (such as frangipane) is then added and the case is to be baked a third time, blind baking times can be reduced as much as half.

You might also want to bake pie-style, with both a top and bottom crust in place. In this case, blind baking is unnecessary. Firstly, ensure your filling is not so moist as to create a soggy bottom – stew or reduce, if needed. And make sure the top is pierced to allow excess moisture out. You'll want to bake a 12-inch tart for at least 40 minutes at 180°C/160°C fan/Gas 4, turning down the temperature if it's browning too fast. Don't stop baking until you are sure the bottom is baked, taking it out to have a look if necessary.

Any top-crusted pie should be glazed with at least a little milk. Ideally, though, you should use egg wash. This is just egg whisked with a pinch of salt to break down the proteins and make it more liquid, and makes for a deep golden glow. For the darkest and shiniest result, glaze with only the egg's yolk.

## VARIATIONS

**EGG**   Adding egg to pastry increases the fat content and thus makes the pastry more difficult to handle, but gives a handsome, rich flavour. Some say only add the yolk; I think this is a good idea if you've got one or two spare, but don't separate an egg for the purpose. In the basic recipe, replace 50g water with one medium egg or three medium yolks. If it's too dry you can top it up with a little water or milk.

**DAIRY**   Adding milk to pastry instead of water will increase both its crumbliness and its richness. You can get creative with yoghurt, sour cream, crème fraîche and all manner of dairy products – replace the water in a ratio of 1:1. Watch out, however, as the dairy product will make the pastry harder to handle (shorter) and the sugar it contains will cause your pastry to brown prematurely.

**CHEESE**   A large handful of Parmesan (or similar) cheese will add a kick to your pastry in quiches and other savouries. For a crumbly and more subtle cheesiness, replace a touch of the liquid with any soft cheese: ricotta and cream cheese work well.

**CITRUS**   Don't use the juice. If you want a subtle citrus hit, grate in a little zest after weighing out the flour and butter.

## SUBSTITUTIONS

FLOUR   You can make your pastry gluten-free quite easily – just replace the plain flour with a gluten-free flour blend (preferably one based on rice flour). You don't need to change the quantities, but you might find you need to add a tad less water with some blends. You do not need to rest gluten-free pastry in the fridge, but the cold will help it hold its shape.

BUTTER   My gran always made pastry with half shortening and half lard. This does eliminate the overall butteriness, but it makes the pastry light and crumbly. You'll need to try it and judge what's best for yourself. In dishes where you want the pastry to occupy more of a background role, try taking out half the butter and replacing it with lard.

## STORAGE

Unfilled pastry cases will keep for several days at room temperature – lightly wrap in cling film and they won't go soggy. As soon as they are filled their crispness will begin to depreciate. The life of your cases, though, will almost certainly be limited by the life of the filling.

Pastry cases freeze magnificently. Wrap them individually in a layer of cling film and freeze, though try to keep them in a little-opened drawer as they are especially brittle when cold.

## TROUBLESHOOTING

*Why has my pastry shrunk?* Two things cause shrinkage: too much gluten formation and not enough resting. Don't overwork your dough and don't add too much water. Make sure to chill your dough in the fridge after you've lined your case. Always leave a little hanging over the edge too, as the gravity can provide enough extra tension to secure it in place.

*Why do I have a soggy bottom?* If your pastry is too thick, it's going to take ages to cook and so will inevitably have a soggy bottom. If you've blind baked, you've not done it for long enough. And if you've baked from raw with a filling, your filling may have been too wet or your dish too substantial. Use a metal tin if you can.

*Why have my sides fallen over?* If your pastry is very short (if it has lots of fat in), it won't support its own weight very well. The same goes for gluten-free pastry. You should try to leave plenty of pastry hanging over the edge, or freeze your pastry in its case before baking.

*Why is my pastry tough and doughy?* Adding too much water is the biggest culprit. Or you've possibly worked it too much. Equally, if your pastry recipe doesn't have enough fat in it, you can end up with tough pastry. Check your butter has a high fat content.

*Why is my pastry impossible to roll?* Be persistent. The harder your pastry is to roll, the crumblier it will be and the better it will taste. If it is too difficult, add more water next time. If you're stuck in the stressful situation of having breaking pastry right now, warming it up will help.

*Why is my pastry unevenly cooked?* Simple – roll it out better.

# ONION TART

MAKES ONE 12-INCH TART

Here we are in that very blurred area between baking and cooking. The question is, if you set a proficient baker and a proficient chef the challenge of creating the best onion tart, who'd win? I'd be willing to bet the baker, so long as she/he didn't forget one thing: seasoning. You need lots of salt and pepper because salt and pepper make things taste nice. The cream will take care of the rest.

There are lots of onions in this recipe. They do not need to be diced finely, just sliced into slivers. When cooking, get a bit of brown on them or you risk the tart being bland.

*1 x quantity basic shortcrust*
  *pastry (see pages 150–153)*
*1kg onions*
*50g unsalted butter*
*2 medium eggs*
*300ml double cream*

*100g Parmesan cheese,*
  *finely grated*
  *(or veggie alternative)*
*sea salt and freshly ground*
  *black pepper*

1. First, make a quantity of basic shortcrust pastry (see page 50). Whilst the pastry is resting in the fridge, preheat the oven to 180°C/160°C fan/Gas 4 and grease a 12-inch tart tin.

2. Roll out your chilled pastry on a floured surface to the thickness of a £1 coin. Roll it up around your rolling pin then unfurl. You should then trim around the edges, leaving at least 1 centimetre overhanging. Prick the case with a fork and chill for another 15 minutes. Freeze any excess pastry.

3. Cover the pastry case with a sheet of baking paper and weight down with coins or baking beans. Bake for 15 minutes covered, then remove the paper and bake for a further 10 minutes uncovered before setting aside until the filling is ready. Once baked, you should trim off any excess pastry with a sharp knife.

4. Whilst the pastry case is baking, make the filling. Chop the onions into thin slices, preferably using a food processor for speed. In a frying pan, melt the butter over a medium heat and add the onions. Fry them until completely soft and just browned – if they're sticking or browning too fast, add some water. If they're not browning at all, add some salt and gradually increase the heat. This will take about 15–20 minutes.

5. Beat the eggs, cream and most of the cheese together in a bowl and add loads of seasoning. Stir in the onions, then scoop this mixture into your blind-baked tart case. Sprinkle with the rest of the cheese and bake for another 25–30 minutes, or until a deep golden brown.

# MUSHROOM & THYME TART
## WITH POACHED EGG
MAKES 4 INDIVIDUAL TARTS, OR ONE 10-INCH DEEP-FILLED TART

Ha! I hear the cries of scorn. This is hardly innovative – there's nothing with a poached egg on top that's *not* going to be awesome!

Obviously. This is a demonstration of that fact. And I'll show you how to make a truly brilliant (and totally easy) poached egg – you'll never look back. This is an awesome starter or lunch, served with the inevitable rocket salad and balsamic glaze.

*1 x quantity basic shortcrust
    pastry (see pages 150–153)
50g dried wild mushrooms,
    optional
1 onion, finely chopped
3 garlic cloves, finely chopped
50g salted butter
a sprig of thyme*

*500g assorted mushrooms,
    sliced
5 medium eggs
200g crème fraîche
plenty of grated Parmesan
sea salt and freshly ground
    black pepper*

1. First, make a quantity of basic shortcrust pastry (see page 150). Whilst the pastry is resting in the fridge, preheat the oven to 180°C/160°C fan/Gas 4 and grease four 4-inch tart tins (or large tin) with plenty of butter. Rehydrate the dried mushrooms in boiled water, if using.

2. Roll out your chilled pastry on a floured surface to the thickness of a £1 coin. Cut out discs a little larger than each of your tart tins, so you can leave about a centimetre of pastry hanging over the edge. Line your tart tins with the pastry, prick with a fork and put in the fridge to chill for another 15 minutes. Freeze any excess pastry.

3. Rip off some squares of baking paper and place these on top of your tart cases, weighting them down with baking beans or loose change. Bake for 10 minutes covered, then remove the paper and bake for another 10 minutes uncovered. They should be crisp, but not fully baked. Trim off the excess with a sharp knife, then set aside until needed.

3. Make your filling while the pastry is resting and baking. Place the onions and garlic in a frying pan with the butter and thyme and fry gently over a medium heat for about 10 minutes to soften and brown. If colouring too fast, add a drop of water.

4. Add the mushrooms to the softened, browned onions, including any drained dried mushrooms, along with plenty of salt and pepper. Cook, uncovered, until the mushrooms look almost sludgy – you want to evaporate the vast majority of their water content.

5. When the mushrooms are done, remove from the heat and discard the sprig of thyme. Stir in 1 egg and the crème fraîche and divide between your pastry cases. Bake for 15–20 minutes, until totally set.

6. Just before the baking time is over, poach the eggs. Bring a large pan of salted water to the boil – add loads of salt, up to 1 tablespoon per litre. Then place the 4 remaining eggs (shells on) into the water. Boil for 1 minute. Remove the eggs, then crack each egg, one at a time, into a wee cup, and use the cup to tip them gently into the water – just remember which one's which. Or crack them into four different cups and put them all in the pan at the same time. Check them regularly by lifting them out with a slotted spoon and giving them a prod. They'll take 3–4 minutes, depending on size.

7. Place your poached eggs on your just-baked tarts and sprinkle with Parmesan, a bit of sea salt and black pepper.

# SPICY PEPPERONI QUICHE

MAKES ONE 12-INCH QUICHE

As I've already explored elsewhere in this book, anything + pizza = awesome. Quiche is a fairly indulgent thing, pizza is definitely an indulgent thing, so why not combine the two for something that bit . . . more? Think of this as quiche, takeaway-style.

Although this recipe is deliciously outlandish, this standard filling can be used to make pretty much any classical quiche. You can replace it with all manner of vegetables (place any watery ones on top), meats and cheeses. Indeed, to make a classic quiche Lorraine, replace the fillings here with chopped, fried lardons and top with a bit of Gruyère.

*1 x quantity basic shortcrust*
  *pastry (see pages 150–153)*
*150g cooked chorizo*
*2 eggs*
*300ml double cream*

*125g mozzarella*
*1 x 50g pack of sliced pepperoni*
*jalapeño peppers, from a jar*
*sea salt and freshly ground*
  *black pepper*

1. First, make a quantity of basic shortcrust pastry (see page 150). Whilst the pastry is resting in the fridge, preheat the oven to 180°C/160°C fan/Gas 4 and grease a 12-inch loose-bottomed metal tart tin with plenty of butter.

2. Roll out your chilled pastry on a floured surface to the thickness of a £1 coin. Roll it up around your rolling pin and place it in the tin. You should then trim around the edges, leaving at least a centimetre overhang. Prick the base with a fork and chill for another 15 minutes. Freeze any excess pastry.

3. Line your pastry case with a torn-off square of baking paper, weighted down with baking beans or loose change. Bake the case for 20–25 minutes, then remove the paper and continue baking for 10 minutes until golden and crisp.

4. Whilst the case is baking, make the filling. Chop the cooked chorizo into rough 1cm squares.

Whisk the eggs and cream together in a jug with some salt and pepper, then add the chorizo. Slice your mozzarella thinly.

5. When your tart case is done, trim off the excess pastry with a sharp knife. Place the case back on your oven shelf and pour your eggy mix into it. Bake for 20 minutes, or until just firming up. Then, lightly place the mozzarella on top, followed by some pepperoni slices and jarred jalapeños. Bake for a final 15 minutes, until the top is a deep golden brown and the filling has completely set.

6. Leave to cool in the tin for 5 minutes before serving with a token salad. It's also excellent cold.

## GRANNY'S APPLE PIE

MAKES ONE 12-INCH PIE

This is the first thing I ever baked. Ever. I was about four, so don't be complaining that this is too difficult for you.

I still remember it clearly – I was stood on a mini-stepladder over at my gran's house, and she let me make a big mess of the pastry. I remember thinking that kneading was imperative, despite her insistence to the contrary, so I would pound and pound it whilst her back was turned. How horrified I am with myself now.

This particular pie is pure – no flourishes. You could add a couple of teaspoons of ground ginger or cinnamon. I quite like to add lavender – it's exquisite and not at all 'a bit knicker drawer', as Sue Perkins once expressed.

And the fruit needn't be apple. Try rhubarb or pear, amongst others. As long as you stew the fruit beforehand, it won't be too soggy.

*200g plain flour, plus extra
    for rolling
50g Stork baking margarine
50g lard, cold*

*4 large Bramley apples
caster sugar, to taste
1 egg, beaten (egg wash)*

1. Preheat your oven to 180°C/160°C fan/Gas 4. Heavily grease a glass pie dish.

2. Into a large bowl, weigh out the plain flour. Add the Stork margarine and lard and use your thumbs and fingers to rub them in until the mixture is the consistency of breadcrumbs. Shake the bowl to bring any lumps to the top.

3. Add a few of teaspoons of ice-cold water and stir with a knife to bring the pastry together. Add more water as needed – it should just come together.

4. Once made, cover your bowl and chill the pastry in the fridge.

5. Peel and chop the apples into small chunks and place them in a pan with a few tablespoons of caster sugar (to taste) and a teaspoon of water. Cook on a medium heat, stirring regularly, until the apples have broken down. They should be thick and hold together, with a few lumps.

6. Divide your pastry into two lumps, one slightly bigger than the other. Roll out your big lump with plenty of flour, constantly turning your pastry 90 degrees for ultimate evenness. Roll it up around your rolling pin and place it in the pie dish, leaving at least a centimetre overhang. Then roll out the smaller lump.

7. Fill your pie dish with stewed apple and brush the egg wash around the edge, so that it acts as a glue between the top and bottom layers of pastry.

8. Top with the second disc of pastry, pressing them together. Use both your thumbs to pinch them together all the way around the edge. Trim off the excess with a knife. Cut a slit in the middle of the pastry to let any moisture out whilst cooking, along with four smaller slits around the edge. Brush the whole thing with egg wash.

9. Bake for 35–45 minutes, until the top is a deep, golden brown and you can see that the base is cooked through the glass. Serve hot or cold, with tinned Ambrosia custard or Walls ice cream. It is perfect at any temperature.

# CHERRY BAKEWELL
MAKES ONE 10-INCH TART

Despite being a sweet tart, Bakewell is a classic that is strictly shortcrust. This is the standard, made with a raspberry compote beneath a thick layer of frangipane, just a bit more awesome. This also has cherries.

Notably, cherries contain the compound benzaldehyde. This is what almond essence is made from and which gives Dr Pepper its main flavour component. But the tiny amounts in both cherries and almonds mean that these flavours blend seamlessly together and that's why this combination is so well loved.

If you've got any frozen cherries left over, make the most awe-inspiring crumble in the world by combining them with some cooking apples (see crumble topping, page 34).

*1 x quantity basic shortcrust
   pastry (see pages 150–153)
2 x quantity frangipane
   (see page 25)
flaked almonds, for
   decoration*

*For the cherry jam*
*150g frozen cherries
150g frozen or fresh
   raspberries
100g caster sugar*

1. First, make a quantity of basic shortcrust pastry (see page 150). Whilst the pastry is resting in the fridge, preheat the oven to 180°C/160°C fan/Gas 4 and grease a 12-inch tart tin with plenty of butter.

2. Roll out your chilled pastry on a floured surface to the thickness of a £1 coin. Roll it up around your rolling pin and place it in the tart tin. You should then trim around the edges, leaving at least a centimetre overhang. Prick the base with a fork and chill for another 15 minutes. Freeze any excess pastry.

3. Line your pastry case with a square of baking paper weighted down with some loose change or some baking beans. Bake for 15–20 minutes, then remove the paper and bake for another 10 minutes until pale, but obviously cooked.

4. Whilst the case is baking, start the jam. Put the cherries and raspberries into a pan with the sugar, place on a high heat and bring to a boil. Reduce the heat to medium and simmer until thick and jammy, stirring regularly. This will take about 10 minutes.

5. Make your frangipane whilst the pastry is baking (see page 25).

6. When the pastry is baked, trim the excess with a sharp knife. Spread your jam over the base and then cover carefully with frangipane. Sprinkle the flaked almonds on top. Return to the oven and bake for 20 minutes or until the frangipane is springy and golden.

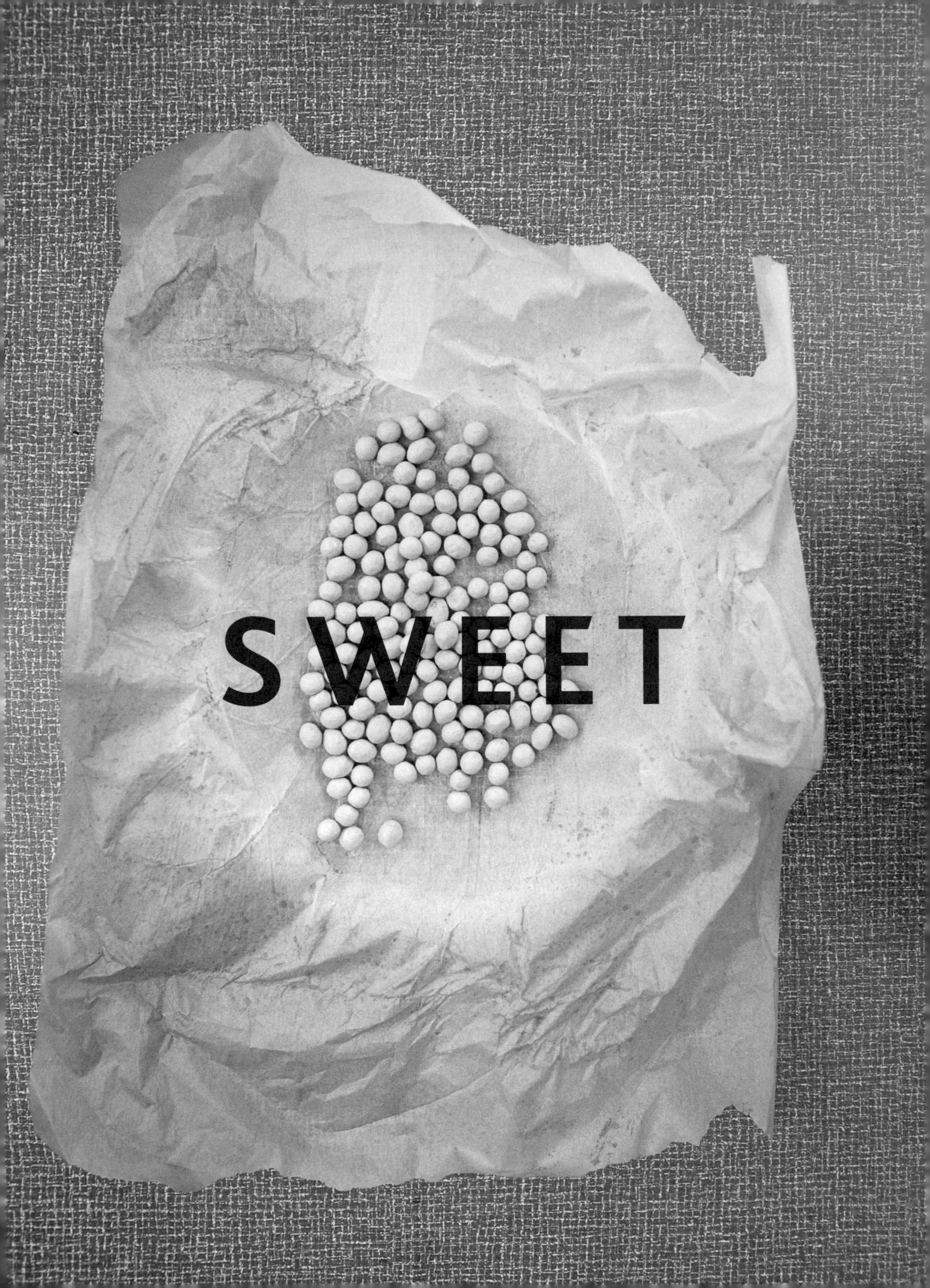

# SWEET

# SWEET

Sweet pastry (sweetcrust) is a type of pastry made with at least flour, butter and sugar. It is used for tarts and sweet pies.

In the UK, there are two basic varieties of pastry: shortcrust and sweetcrust. In France, sweet pastry is further split into pâte sucrée and pâte sablée. Pâte sucrée is created with the addition of caster sugar to a shortcrust pastry mix; pâte sablée uses icing sugar and is heavily enriched, making it more snappy and biscuit-like. The basic recipe given in this chapter is a good compromise between both.

To make sweet pastry the traditional English way, follow the guide in the shortcrust pastry section using the ingredients below. But I like to turn everything on its head. Don't start by rubbing the flour and almost-frozen butter together; that way, you're developing gluten from the start. Instead, use room temperature butter, cream it with the sugar and egg as you would for a cake, then incorporate the flour at the end before chilling.

Bear in mind, though, that the rigid rules that apply to shortcrust pastry also apply to sweet. Their snubbing will not result in such a disastrous result, but you shouldn't add too much liquid or work the pastry too hard.

## THE IDEAL SWEETCRUST PASTRY

The sweet pastry case can be any shape or size. It should never be more than 5mm thick. The pastry of smaller tarts should be only just thick enough to maintain structural integrity. The edges should be trimmed and straight, the colour a pale to golden brown and never burnt. There should be no holes or gaps.

When broken, the pastry should snap with light crumbling. It should not be hard or tough, but should not be overly crumbly either. It should not be cloying or gummy in the mouth and should never leave the mouth dry. It should be sweet, though not overly so, and never bitter. And it should never, ever have a soggy bottom.

## BASIC SWEETCRUST PASTRY RECIPE
MAKES ONE LARGE PASTRY CASE

*125g salted butter, at room temperature*
*75g icing sugar*
*1 medium egg*
*a dash of vanilla extract, optional*
*250g plain flour*

### GREASE

Grease your tart tin with lots of butter. Don't use baking paper. Your tin should be loose bottomed and made of metal.

### WHY

Pastry tries to stick to the tin, and sweet pastry tries doubly hard, so do everything you can to stop it. As for your tin choice – ideally go for metal. Ceramic or stone dishes have no place in your baking life; they don't transfer the heat from the oven very well and you'll end up with a soggy bottom.

### BEAT

Into a large bowl, weigh the butter and icing sugar. Beat them together with an electric mixer or wooden spoon until soft and pliable.

### WHY

By creaming, you're not trying to tear little air holes in the butter, as you are when making a cake. This is why you must use blunt icing sugar in this method. You only want to soften the mix to facilitate the introduction of the egg.

### EGG

Add the egg and vanilla, if using. Beat until the mixture is smooth.

### WHY

Again, you're not wanting to incorporate air here, so don't go crazy. Beat it as little as possible, just until the mixture is homogeneous.

### FOLD

Add the flour and fold it in with a large spoon, switching to your hands when necessary. Be as gentle as you can.

### REST

Wrap your pastry in cling film and rest it in the fridge for at least half an hour, and preferably overnight.

### ROLL

Carefully roll out your pastry. I'd use cling film for this: lay a sheet out flat on a work surface, plonk your unwrapped pastry on top and lay another sheet of cling film on top. Roll out until it is no thicker than a £1 coin, and even front to back. Crouch down to the pastry's level to check. You can also use two sheets of baking paper to great effect

### WHY

It's important to stop the gluten developing. Overworking can result in jaw-crushing pastry. Only work it enough to just incorporate the flour into the liquid.

### WHY

This allows the gluten that's been developed to relax and not be so problematic. Chilled pastry won't stick so badly when rolling out, and chilling will also stop any nasty bugs growing in it.

### WHY

Rolling reactivates the gluten and arranges it all in a flat formation. So to avoid shrunken, tough pastry, you want to do this as gently and gradually as possible. Cling film stops the incorporation of excess flour (this can also make the pastry dry and tough) and alleviates any problems with sticking.

### PATCH AND PRICK

Peel off the top layer of cling film and transfer the pastry to your tin (cutting out if necessary) and tuck in carefully. It is OK to patch any areas looking a bit perforated. Always leave at least a centimetre hanging over the edge. Prick the pastry all over with a fork. If you have any leftover pastry, use it for jam tarts.

### CHILL

Finally, chill your pastry case for at least a further 15 minutes before baking.

### WHY

Pricking the pastry stops it puffing up in the oven. I think of it like pitta breads and naan breads. Pitta breads you don't prick and they puff up like balloons. Naan breads you stab and they stay flat. And so long as you patch your holes well, your mixture will melt slightly and weld any rough edges together in the oven.

### WHY

This will calm and soothe the gluten you've just riled up through rolling, giving a better snap, a little crumble and not so much shrinkage.

## THE BAKE

For the vast majority of dishes involving sweet pastry, blind baking is required. Sweet pastry does not hold its shape well, so it is difficult to use it for closed pies with moist fillings. If you do decide to bake closed, do so with a filling that's relatively dry and stable.

To blind bake, preheat your oven to 180°C/160°C fan/Gas 4. Tear off a large square of baking paper and place it on top of your chilled tart case. Weight it down with some change, preferably coppers – I tend to use whatever's in my pocket. You can use baking beans, but these don't transfer heat as rapidly as metal coins. Bake for 20–25 minutes for a large tart case, or for 10–15 minutes for smaller individual cases. Then remove the paper and weights and check for any wee holes or shrinkage. Use any leftover scraps of pastry to plug them. Return to the oven and bake for at least another 10 minutes to brown and crisp. If your recipe requires baking one more time, as many do, the filling should prevent the pastry from browning any more.

## VARIATIONS

CHOCOLATE  To make a pastry chocolatey, all you've got to do is add a wee bit of cocoa powder. Adding 50g to the basic recipe with the flour will work brilliantly. Add some chocolate extract in place of the vanilla to take the flavour to the next level.

NUTS  Recipes for pâte sablée often include the addition of ground almonds. In fact, you can use any nuts you like – these will add to the crumbliness but reduce the demographic of your pastry enjoyment somewhat, due to those annoying allergies. If using, replace a quarter of the flour in your pastry recipe with ground nuts. Pistachios and hazelnuts work particularly well.

SPICES  Cinnamon is my favourite spice to sneak into pastry. This works well with any homely, spicy recipe, especially traditional southern US recipes involving pumpkins, sweet potatoes or apples. I'd add two teaspoons of spice to the recipe above with the flour. Please, experiment with whatever you've got in the cupboard!

BAKING POWDER  In some Italian recipes (including the Torta Della Nonna recipe on page 178), many bakers will add a bit of baking powder to the pastry to make it more cake-like. Don't add more than a teaspoon.

## SUBSTITUTIONS

FLOUR  In any pastry recipe, flour can be replaced 1:1 with a gluten-free plain flour blend – rice-flour-based products work best. A proportion of the flour can be replaced with ground nuts, but you cannot get away with substituting more than about 30 per cent.

BUTTER  Butter can be replaced with shortening (hard margarine) or lard, but it doesn't taste of very much – just 'sweet'. Stick to butter if you can. Vegan substitutes are common in supermarkets. But they're vegan.

EGG  Eggs can be replaced with pretty much any liquid. The average medium egg weighs up to about 50g (shell off), so just replace the egg with 50g of liquid. Milk, water and single cream all work well. For a richer flavour and darker colour, and a pastry that can be rather difficult to work, replace the whole egg with three egg yolks. Top your filling with meringue to use up those spare whites.

SUGAR  Sweet pastry should not be made with sweetener, *ever*. It is the biscuity snap provided by the sugar that is an essential part of its form. You can use caster sugar or any finely ground or soft brown sugar if you don't have icing sugar, but don't beat too hard. You should never use granulated.

EXTRACTS AND ESSENCES  All kinds of aromatics work particularly well in sweet pastry; not just vanilla as mentioned above. You can replace it with a slug of rosewater, a dab of orange flower, a blast of almond extract or even a shot of espresso.

## STORAGE

The important thing is to remove your pastry from any kind of humidity lest it become soggy cardboard. Once completely cooled, store it in the fridge in an airtight container, or wrapped in cling film. It will usually stay crisp for up to four days.

Empty cases freeze well. Wrap them individually in a layer of cling film and freeze, though try to keep them in a drawer to themselves as they are especially brittle when cold.

Equally, the dough freezes beautifully – as you might imagine, seeing as you can buy it frozen in the shops. Keep it wrapped to stop it drying out, and defrost overnight before using.

# TROUBLESHOOTING

*Why do the walls of the case collapse during baking?* Your pastry is too short, too warm, or you haven't left enough excess hanging over the side of your tin. By short, I mean that it has too much fat to support its own weight – my recipe contains an egg, which can cause this problem. The solution is to leave excess pastry hanging over the edge and to properly chill (even freeze) the pastry case before baking.

*Why has my pastry shrunk?* Either too much gluten formation or not enough resting. Both can be solved with extra resting time in the fridge. Try not to overwork your dough and please don't add any more water than you need to. Make sure to chill your dough in the fridge after you've rolled it out and lined your case. Always leave a little hanging over the edge, as gravity can provide enough tension to keep it still. To test if it is ready for baking, stretch a bit of the overhanging pastry – if it springs back, rest it for longer. If it stretches and stays, it's ready to bake.

*Why has my sweet pastry burnt?* It is simply very easy to burn sweet pastry. Make sure that during the first blind bake your sides are properly covered with paper. Make sure, too, that you've rolled out the pastry completely flat, as thinner areas will rise in temperature much faster and so burn quicker. Ultimately, turn down your oven if it is a regular problem.

*Why is my pastry gummy or cardboard?* This is usually down to a combination of overworking and adding too much liquid. I think of this result as a flattened bread crust that's a bit sweet. When making pastry you need to do the opposite of what you do when making bread: add as little water as possible and mix the dough only just enough to bring everything together.

*Why is my bottom soggy?* Simple – you've not baked it enough, or your pastry is so thick that it takes a ridiculously long time to bake (so you've not baked it enough). Turn your oven down by 20°C and bake for longer. Make sure your pastry is no thicker than a £1 coin.

# FRANGIPANE FRUIT TART

MAKES ONE 10-INCH TART

This is as easy as tart-baking gets – even simpler than the ever-so-simple Glazed Fruit Tart (see page 176). All you need is pastry, frangipane, fruit. Maybe a bit of jam if you wanna go all crazy on us.

There's no blind baking involved because the frangipane itself will weigh down the bottom of your tart without causing a soggy bottom. You can add the fruit before or after baking – it's up to you. I'd go before, just because of the way the frangipane will rise up around it.

*1 x quantity basic sweetcrust pastry (see pages 168–171)*
*1 x quantity frangipane (see page 25)*
*jam of your chosen fruit (from a jar or see page 35), optional*

*fresh fruit, such as raspberries, sliced peaches, blackberries, sliced apples, cherries*
*icing sugar, for dusting*

1. First, make a quantity of basic sweetcrust pastry (see page 168). It's best made the night before. Whilst the pastry is resting in the fridge, preheat the oven to 170°C/150°C fan/Gas 3 and grease a 10-inch loose-bottomed tart tin.

2. Roll out your chilled pastry on a floured surface to the thickness of a £1 coin. Cut out a pastry disc, making sure it's slightly bigger than your tin, and line your tin. Because this is baked already filled, trim your pastry to the edge now – you're relying on your pastry-making skills for it not to shrink. Prick the base then chill your case in the fridge.

3. Make your frangipane whilst the pastry is chilling (see page 25).

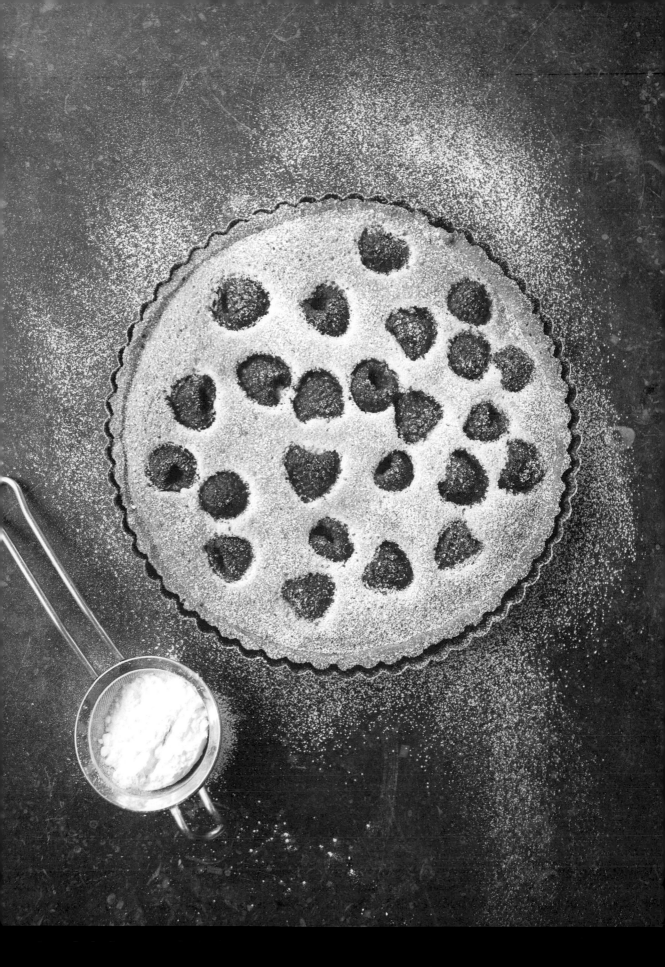

4. Spread a generous layer of jam all over your base, if using. Then carefully spread the frangipane over the top. Finally drop your fruit sporadically over the top.

5. Bake your tart for 30–35 minutes, or until golden brown and glorious. Leave to cool in the tin, then remove the sides by standing your loose-bottomed tin on top of an upturned pudding bowl. Just before serving, dust the tart with icing sugar.

# GLAZED FRUIT TART

MAKES ONE 10-INCH TART, OR 6 INDIVIDUAL TARTS

This is a wee step up from the Frangipane Fruit Tart (see page 174), but still really easy to make stunning – all it takes is pastry, crème pat and fruit, all of which can be prepared in advance and assembled at your leisure. To get that shine, I tend to use some shop-bought apricot jam.

The most traditional glazed tarts involve strawberries, raspberries, blueberries or blackberries. You can use anything you like; the only condition is that it looks pretty.

One final twist is to combine this recipe and the Frangipane Fruit Tart – rather than blind baking the pastry case, cover it with frangipane. Then add crème pat and fresh fruit. It just adds another dimension.

*1 x quantity basic sweetcrust pastry (see pages 168–171)*
*1 x quantity crème pâtissière (see page 23)*

*fresh fruit, such as blueberries, strawberries or raspberries*
*apricot jam*

1. First, make a quantity of basic sweetcrust pastry (see page 168). It's best made the night before. Whilst the pastry is resting in the fridge, preheat the oven to 180°C/160°C fan/Gas 4 and grease a 10-inch loose-bottomed tart tin (or six 4-inch tart tins).

2. Roll out your chilled pastry on a floured surface to the thickness of a £1 coin. Cut out a disc bigger than your greased tart tin, so that there's a centimetre or so hanging over the edge, and line the tin. Prick the case with a fork and chill for another 10 minutes.

3. Cover the pastry case with a sheet of baking paper, weighting it down with baking beans or some loose change. Bake in the oven for 15–20 minutes, then remove the paper and bake for another 10–15 minutes until golden brown and crisp. Trim off the excess pastry with a sharp knife and set aside until ready.

4. Make the crème pat whilst the pastry is baking (see page 23). You can either pour it, still warm and gloopy, into your pastry case and leave it to set, or you can pipe it in once it's set. I'll leave this up to you.

5. When your crème pat is moderately set, decorate your tarts with fruit. Do this as you will – my favourite method is to add a big pile of fruit, leaving little crème pat visible.

6. Finally, to glaze, heat a few tablespoons of the apricot jam in a pan with a few tablespoons of water, stirring to amalgamate. Brush the resulting hot syrup over your fruit for a glossy effect.

# TORTA DELLA NONNA
## (GRANDMOTHER'S TART)
### MAKES ONE 10-INCH TART

This is an Italian custard tart that is magnificent in its simplicity. I first had it pretty recently, at a wee café in Glasgow. This café (Smile is the name) is more Italian than you would have thought possible in Glasgow. Indeed, the language echoes off the postcard-covered walls. I often go in for the legendary sandwiches, but they also have a load of very traditional and quite rustic-looking tarts on display.

'Pine nut and custard tart' didn't sound that appealing, but I thought I'd give it a go. I was so wrong to doubt it. It is amazing. It's perfect. And so simple. Please, please, please, just give it a try. You'll be converted for life.

If you don't like the sound of ricotta, try making this tart with a filling of crème pat (see page 23) flavoured with the zest of a lemon. Top with pastry, then coat in pine nuts and icing sugar.

*1 x quantity basic sweetcrust
  pastry (see pages 168–171)
500g ricotta
juice and zest of 1 lemon*

*200g icing sugar
3 egg yolks
150g pine nuts
icing sugar, for dusting*

1. First, make a quantity of basic sweetcrust pastry (see page 168). It's best made the night before. Whilst the pastry is resting in the fridge, preheat the oven to 170°C/150°C fan/Gas 3 and grease a 10-inch loose-bottomed tart tin.

2. Into a large bowl, weigh the ricotta, lemon juice and zest, icing sugar, egg yolks and half the pine nuts. Mix to combine well – do not mix to incorporate air.

3. Divide your pastry into two lumps, one slightly bigger than the other. Roll out your big lump with plenty of flour to the thickness of a £1 coin, and use this to line your greased tin. Scoop in all the filling. Then roll out the second lump and lay this over the top, pressing the pastry together. Use both your thumbs to pinch them together all the way around the edge. Trim off the excess with a knife.

4. Scatter the top with the rest of your pine nuts, then bake your tart for 40–45 minutes or until golden on top. The colour of the pine nuts will give you a better indication than the pastry on whether it's done. When baked, leave to cool to room temperature before serving. Once it has cooled, dust liberally with icing sugar.

# TARTELETTES AU CITRON MERINGUÉE

MAKES 6 INDIVIDUAL TARTS OR ONE 10-INCH TART

The reason I haven't included a standard lemon meringue pie recipe in this book is because a quick google will return hundreds of recipes that are exceptional. You can use the guides on shortcrust pastry (see pages 150–153) and meringue (see pages 220–222) to help you improve them.

This recipe, on the other hand, is for a special occasion or for a seriously impressive bake sale contribution. It's made with thin and snappy sweet pastry, proper tarte au citron filling and a delicate Italian meringue topping. In other words, this is posh lemon meringue pie. And superior in every way. How could it not be, with that many eggs involved?

To make a classic tarte au citron, simply leave out the meringue and add half a tub (about 150ml) of double cream to your filling mixture before baking.

1 x quantity basic sweetcrust
   pastry (see pages 168–171)

**For the filling**
juice and zest of 6 large lemons
5 eggs, plus 4 egg yolks
250g caster sugar
60g butter

**For the Italian meringue**
4 egg whites
200g caster sugar
50g water

1. First, make a quantity of basic sweetcrust pastry (see page 168). Whilst the pastry is resting in the fridge, preheat the oven to 180°C/160°C fan/Gas 4 and grease six 4-inch loose-bottomed tartlet tins (or one 10-inch tin).

2. Roll out your chilled pastry on a floured surface to the thickness of a £1 coin. Cut out discs a little larger than each of your tart tins – I use a pudding bowl as a cutter – so there's about a centimetre of pastry hanging over the edge. Line your tart tins with the pastry, prick with a fork and put in the fridge to chill for another 10 minutes.

3. Tear off squares of baking paper and place these on top of your tart cases, weighting them down with baking beans or loose change. Bake for 15 minutes covered, then remove the paper and bake for another 10 minutes or until crisp and golden. Leave to cool, cutting off any excess pastry with a sharp knife.

4. Whilst they're baking, make the filling. Place the lemon juice and zest in a pan. Add the eggs, yolks and sugar and place on a medium heat, whisking all the time. You want to cook the mixture to thicken it, without causing the eggs to scramble. Control the heat carefully; it should not boil.

5. When your mix feels heavy on the whisk and is noticeably thicker (at about 75°C on a thermometer), remove from the heat and (still whisking) add the butter and stir to melt.

6. Pour your mix into your tartlet cases, then place them back in the oven, turning the temperature down to 120°C/100°C fan/Gas ½. Bake for 15 minutes, then leave to cool whilst you make the meringue.

7. Into a large clean bowl (not plastic or silicone), place the egg whites. With an electric mixer (or using a stand mixer), whisk on a high speed until they're big and fluffy and not getting any bigger. At the same time, place the sugar and water in a pan together and bring to a boil. Bubble furiously for about a minute (at 118°C if you have a thermometer), before drizzling slowly into your egg whites whilst continuing to whisk on the highest speed.

8. Load your Italian meringue into a piping bag with a nozzle of your choice. Pipe little peaks all over your tarts to cover them, then use a blowtorch to brown them. Alternatively, place them in a very hot oven for 5–10 minutes. Serve once cooled.

# CHOCOLATE CARAMEL TARTLETS
MAKES 6 INDIVIDUAL TARTS, OR ONE 10-INCH TART

Maybe you're starting to get an idea of how this baking thing works. How a professional patissière makes all the hundreds of different bakes every day. For the tarts? They need one massive batch of pastry. One massive batch of crème pat. One massive batch of frangipane. The rest is just assembly.

And here it continues – this is an amazing tart, often touted as 'chocolate and *salted* caramel tart'. And what is it? It's just pastry, caramel sauce (page 28) and chocolate ganache (see page 30). For us at home, these are easy things to make in advance if we need to. I believe its unadorned finish is its beauty. I can't think of anything to top it without ruining it slightly.

1 x quantity basic sweetcrust
   pastry (see pages 168–171)
2 x quantity easy caramel
   sauce (see page 28)

*For the chocolate ganache*
300g good dark chocolate
300g double cream

1. First, make a quantity of basic sweetcrust pastry (see page 168). It's best made the night before. Whilst the pastry is resting in the fridge, preheat the oven to 180°C/160°C fan/ Gas 4 and grease six loose-bottomed tartlet tins.

2. Roll out your chilled pastry on a floured surface to the thickness of a £1 coin. Cut out discs a little larger than each of your tart tins – I use a pudding bowl as a cutter – so there's about a centimetre of pastry hanging over the edge. Line your tart tins with the pastry, prick with a fork and put in the fridge to chill for another 10 minutes.

3. Tear off squares of baking paper and place these on top of your tart cases, weighting them down with baking beans or loose change. Bake for 15 minutes covered, then remove the paper and bake for another 10 minutes or until crisp and golden. Leave to cool, cutting off any excess pastry with a sharp knife.

4. Make the caramel sauce (see page 28). Half fill each case with the caramel sauce and leave to set in the fridge.

5. Finally, make the ganache (see page 30 for a more comprehensive guide). Break the chocolate into little chunks and place in a bowl. Bring your cream to the boil in a saucepan over a medium heat, then pour over your chocolate and stir to combine. Pour this over your caramel and chill your tarts before serving.

CHOUX

# CHOUX

Choux pastry (*pâte à choux*) is a light dough made from butter, liquid (milk or water), eggs and flour that, once baked, gives us profiteroles, éclairs, and their various sweet and savoury assemblages and adaptations, from Paris-Brest to cheese puffs. A hotly debated point of baking semantics, choux (French for 'cabbages') probably gets its name from the appearance of the baked buns. I have, for years, fronted a campaign to change the name to '*pâte à sprouts*'.

Choux is the only pastry that is cooked twice, as it is first heated on the hob and then baked. It has a reputation for being tricky, requiring you to judge the amount of egg white to add at the end, which in turn depends on how long you spent drying out your dough on the hob; the drier your dough and the more egg you incorporate, the more puff you'll get in the oven. Yet choux isn't complicated at all. A passable choux pastry can be made with the most reckless of recipes, and a brilliant one with just a wee bit of care. Following the step by step and understanding *why* we do *what* we do can turn around the most floundering of home bakers.

## THE IDEAL CHOUX PASTRY

The final choux bun should be vastly bigger than the equivalent raw dough – at least 3–4 times – and should not shrink after baking. It should be an even golden brown colour on both bottom and top, and can be glazed or unglazed. A rustic, irregular rise is acceptable and often desired.

When cut, the centre should be entirely hollow and the walls a mere 1–2mm thick. The buns should be light and crisp – they should not be soggy. The taste should be buttery, almost savoury, and contrast with the fillings or toppings used.

## BASIC CHOUX PASTRY RECIPE

**MAKES 12–18 CHOUX BUNS OR ÉCLAIRS**

*150g milk*
*50g salted butter*
*80g strong white flour*

*2 medium eggs, plus*
*1–3 medium egg whites*

  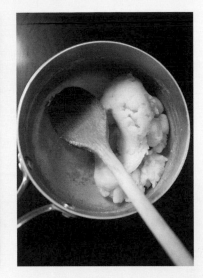

### BOIL

Line a baking tray with baking paper. Weigh the milk and butter into a saucepan and place on a high heat until boiling.

### FLOUR

Remove the pan from the heat, add the flour and stir to combine.

### STIR, LOTS

Reduce the heat to medium, return the pan to the heat, and stir vigorously with a wooden spoon for several minutes. It will become smoother and well combined. You want to keep going until, although you're still stirring, it is sticking to the bottom of the pan.

### WHY

You need to heat the liquid so that when you add the flour, it doesn't form into clumps, then a stodgy mess, and then burn as it heats up. Nasty.

### WHY

This is simply for the formation of the dough – it will look like a horrible mess. Don't worry; this is what you want.

### WHY

Here, you are cooking the starch and 'denaturing' the protein in the flour, so don't worry about overmixing. You are also drying out the mixture by evaporating the liquid, allowing you to add more egg for a greater final puff.

### COOL

Once your dough is suitably dry, you need to cool it to the extent that you see no more steam rising from the bowl. This can take a bit of time, depending on your batch size; I beat it with an electric mixer to speed the cooling process significantly.

### EGGS

When no more steam is rising from the pan/bowl, add the whole eggs, one at a time. After each addition, beat the mixture until totally smooth. Using an electric mixer makes things easier.

### DROPPING

The final choux mix should be of a similar consistency to a rubbery, glossy cake mix – it should fall from your spoon/beaters if you shake them, but shouldn't quite flow freely. If it isn't at this stage, beat in the egg whites, one at a time, checking the consistency after each addition. Keep going until it's about right.

### WHY

If you were to add the eggs at this point, you risk having scrambled egg in your choux. Just like stirring a cup of tea, beating the mixture will cool it quicker.

### WHY

You're beating both air and liquid into the mixture. The more you beat, the more your buns will rise in the oven. The eggs are an emulsifier – this means they bind with both fat and liquid to hold your buns together.

### WHY

This is the right balance between too dry and too wet, giving an excellent rise in the oven without a flat structure and an overly flaky, dry texture. If for some reason your mixture isn't at this stage, add another egg white.

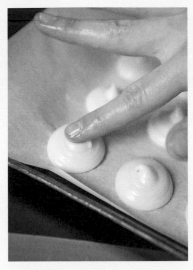

### LUMPS

Make the buns by spooning the mix onto your lined tray; alternatively, scoop your mix into a piping bag with a 1cm hole cut in the end and pipe onto the tray.

### BLUNT

Push the wee point or 'tail' that piping may leave with a wet finger to make the top smooth.

### GLAZE

Glaze with egg wash (a mixture of egg and a pinch of salt), if desired.

### WHY

Piping is better for evenness and for creating elaborate shapes. Many people prefer to scoop for its more rustic finish.

### WHY

This avoids the possibility of the point catching in the oven and burning. The heat penetrates this area first because it is higher up and has a greater surface area.

### WHY

This gives a beautiful shine – the protein in the egg causes more Maillard (browning) reactions and the fats from the yolk give a nice shine.

## THE BAKE

Choux presents us with an interesting predicament: the oven should be hot enough to give the pastry a good rise, but the dough needs to remain in the oven for a long time in order to dry out and become crisp. In order to get the best of both worlds, bake at 200°C/180°C fan/Gas 6 for the first 10 minutes, then reduce the temperature to 170°C/150°C fan/Gas 3 for a final 15–20 minutes to dry it out. Do not open the oven door whilst baking. Some types of choux need different temperatures – for larger buns or a huge showstopper Paris-Brest, for example, turn the oven down 10°C for the second part and bake for a wee bit longer (5–15 minutes).

Baking choux causes it to puff up in the oven – this is because the liquid you've beaten into the mix expands and turns to steam as it is heated. This steam is actually a bit annoying because, well, it's wet. It causes the insides of the buns to be soggy if it's left inside, and if you bake too many buns at a time the outside will never properly crisp up. As soon as you've baked your shapes, it is important to pierce them all in a discreet place to let the steam out.

## VARIATIONS

**SHAPES** The buns can be just about any shape you can imagine or have the skill to pipe out. I recommend bicycles.

**CHEESE** Beat some hard grated cheese into the mix after the eggs for a savoury canapé base; I use a combination of whatever's in the fridge (usually Cheddar and Parmesan).

**SWEET** For a sweeter, snappier choux, add a teaspoon or two of sugar to your milk. Be careful though, for your choux can burn very quickly and end up soggy in the middle. To prevent this, turn your oven down an extra 20°C for the final bake.

**HEALTHY** To make things healthier, the only thing I would change about the preceding recipe is the size of your piping nozzle. Smaller treats are just as satisfying as larger ones, and they give you a chance to practise your technique on each one.

**SPRINKLES** After glazing with a bit of egg wash, I'd recommend sprinkling a little nibbed sugar (sweet) or sea salt (savoury) over your buns for a bit of texture.

## SUBSTITUTIONS

**FLOUR** Plain flour and strong flour can both be used in choux pastry. Plain flour will give a more delicate, crumbly final product, whereas strong flour will create a more snappy, crispy finish. It's up to you, but I prefer to use strong flour. I feel it helps the pastry cope with wetter fillings better. Self-raising flour will also work, but the raising agent in it is useless.

**LIQUID**  You can use water or milk or a combination of the two. Milk gives a richer, darker final pastry, but it is easier to burn. Water is the more traditional liquid used.

**EGGS**  If you don't want to waste an extra egg white or two to slacken the mixture to the desired consistency, choux will work perfectly well with a little extra milk instead.

**BUTTER**  Replacing the butter with baking margarine or shortening will also work, but you shouldn't; for me, the whole point of choux is its buttery taste. I've used salted butter, but you can use unsalted and a pinch of salt instead.

## STORAGE

Fresh choux does not store well and ideally should not be kept in the fridge – this causes it to go both soggy and a little cardboardy. Therefore, it should be used as soon as possible after baking.
      You can freeze choux, however, both baked and unbaked. Open-freeze the mix after it has been piped, and once solid gather it into a bag and store. You can bake from frozen using the same baking instructions above. Or freeze your baked, unfilled buns in freezer bags or cling film, baking for 5 minutes in the oven before using.

## TROUBLESHOOTING

*Why has my choux shrunk?* It's all about the steam that's produced when you bake. You simply need to bake for longer to dry it out, then make sure to prick a hole in every bun to let any residual steam out.

*Why is my choux soggy?*  See above; usually you just need to bake it for longer. If it's getting to the stage where it's nearly burnt, turn the oven down by a good amount (20–30°C) and slowly dry it out. Many fillings also cause choux to be soggy – if you're filling with whipped cream or a soft custard, for example, do so just before serving.

*Why didn't my choux puff up?* The most likely explanation is not enough beating when mixing in the egg (or indeed, not enough egg). It's important to beat thoroughly, and to a dropping consistency – try using an electric mixer. Another possible problem is that your oven isn't hot enough; many have inaccurate gauges. Always, always preheat, and try turning up the heat by 10°C for the first 10 minutes.

*Why is my choux an odd shape?* For a more even rise, pipe instead of spooning. If your choux is splaying everywhere or has lots of tears, it's likely that your dough's texture was too wet or too dry, respectively. Aim for that glossy, dropping consistency.

5. Whilst they're baking, you can concentrate on creating nice bicycle shapes. If you want to miss this out, that's fine. Draw a bicycle frame on a piece of paper, then trace it several times onto baking paper. Make a 2mm hole in the end of the other piping bag, then pipe onto your patterns. Bake these for a few minutes (until golden) whilst your choux tyres are in the oven.

6. When your choux is out of the oven, prick the bottom of each bun with a sharp knife to let any steam out, then leave to cool. Meanwhile, make the Italian meringue buttercream (see page 33) and caramel sauce (see page 28).

7. Once cooled and you have all the bits ready, cut each choux bun in half horizontally. Pipe the Italian meringue buttercream in little peaks around the ring, then top with the caramel sauce, letting it drip down the side. Finally, top off each set of choux tyres with a choux bicycle, embellishing with caramel spokes, if you wish.

# CHOUX DIVORCÉS

MAKES AROUND 15 CHOUX DIVORCES

This is a nice twist on the standard choux bun and gives you something that's really very fancy but with minimal effort. You only need one batch of choux for both buns, one batch of crème pat split in two for the filling, and one batch of glaze split in two for the top.

Ah yes, about that glaze. Is it a faff? Yes. Not everyone's got gelatine hanging around, but it's really cool. Look how shiny it is! Alternatively, make a gloopy icing out of icing sugar and just-boiled water, divide it in two and add coffee to one half and cocoa to the other.

*1 x quantity basic choux pastry buns (see pages 186–189)*

**For the fillings**
*1 x quantity crème pâtissière (see page 23)*
*1 teaspoon instant coffee, dissolved in 1 teaspoon water*
*1 heaped teaspoon cocoa powder*

**For the glazes**
*1 leaf of gelatine*
*120g caster sugar*
*30g golden syrup*
*30g double cream*
*30g cold water*
*½ teaspoon instant coffee*
*30g cocoa powder*

**For the whipped cream**
*200g double cream*
*caster sugar and vanilla extract, to taste*

1. Make the crème pat first (see page 23) and divide it into two bowls. Then, hot or cold, stir the dissolved coffee into one and the cocoa powder into the other. Mix each one to combine – you can't overmix.

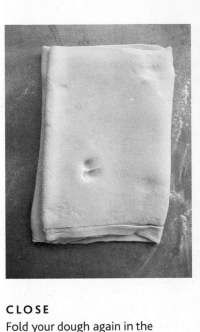

### CLOSE

Fold your dough again in the middle, to close it like a book (this is a book fold).

### WHY

You have doubled your number of layers again. Each time you complete this step, you multiply your layers by four.

**FOLD**

Fold your dough over the butter, then pinch the dough together around the edges to seal the butter in.

**WHY**

You now have one layer of butter encased within two layers of dough. From now on, only think about the layers of butter; ignore the dough.

3. Peel and core the apples, then cut into quarters, then cut each quarter in half again to get eight slices from one apple. Set aside – they may go brown and dry out slightly, but they'll hold their shape better.

4. Weigh out the sugar, butter, water and lemon juice into a frying pan, and heat until the sugar has dissolved and the butter has melted, always stirring.

5. Add the apples so they cover the whole pan and bubble furiously for about 15 minutes, or until the sauce and apples are nicely caramelised to the point of being nearly burnt.

6. Whilst the apples are bubbling, roll out the pastry to the thickness of a £1 coin, using lots of flour. Place the tartlet tins or ramekins upside down on your pastry and cut around them with a knife. You can re-roll any scraps, but obviously the puff won't be quite as even.

7. When the apples are ready, divide them equally into your tart tins. Then, place your cutout discs of pastry on top and tuck them in. Place the tins on the baking tray and bake for about 35 minutes – the pastry should be a deep, dark golden brown and well puffed up. As soon as they are cool enough to handle, turn them upside-down so the apples are on top, remove the tin and serve. Excellent hot or cold.

# CHEAT'S PEAR TARTE TATIN

MAKES ONE LARGE TARTE TATIN

I felt compelled to include a second tarte Tatin recipe because it isn't a traditional tarte Tatin at all. It's the cheat's way to an amazing result. The disadvantage to this method is the length of time it takes, but both the pastry and pears can be prepared in advance.

If you like truly astonishing fruit flavour and perfect pastry, with no added sugar, you can try this. One of the best tartes Tatin I have ever eaten was a blatant cheat. I knew this wee patisserie in the small lake village of Huelgoat in western Brittany was up to something when pannier-transported pastry split during the journey, with the apples coming away from the pastry. They'd definitely cut strips of puff pastry and baked these on a tray. Then they'd cooked the apples down to make a slab, sliced this and placed it on top.

An easy way to replicate this at home is to make a terrine of pure, sliced fruit by baking it in a lined loaf tin until compressed to a dense slab, before marrying it with the puff pastry. Guaranteed perfect pastry and flavour-packed fruit, and so much of it that you don't need to add any extra sugar. You can use apples as is convention, but I'm using pears because I believe the resulting flavour is far more intense.

*½ x quantity puff pastry (see pages 202–205), or a block of shop-bought all-butter puff*

*12 pears, peeled*
*30g unsalted butter*
*1 teaspoon vanilla extract*

OPPOSITE: WEE TARTES TATIN

1. Preheat your oven to 180°C/160°C fan/Gas 4. Grease and line a 2lb loaf tin or 9-inch cake tin with baking paper – if you want a neat finish, cut separate pieces for the bottom and sides. Then grease the paper.

2. Make and rest a quantity of basic puff pastry (see page 202). You'll only need half, so you can either make two tarts or freeze the rest. At the same time, start to prepare the pear terrine, due to the several hours this takes to bake.

3. Core the pears and carefully chop them into thin slices (if you've got a food processor or a mandoline, you could use that). Stack all the pear slices into your tin, pushing them in tightly.

4. Melt the butter in a pan, then remove from the heat and add the vanilla extract and mix. Drizzle this onto the sliced pears, then cover the tin with foil. Place in the oven and bake for an hour. If your tin has any gaps in it, line the bottom of your oven with foil.

5. After an hour, take the pears out of the oven and remove the foil. Use a spatula or a big spoon to compress them firmly. Place a piece of baking paper on top of the pears and put them back in the oven – you want to bake for at least another hour or so. By this time, they'll be caramelised and coloured. Leave them to cool and set.

6. Roll out the puff pastry with plenty of flour to the thickness of a £1 coin. Then, cut around the tin that you baked the pears in, or cut to its rough size if the tin is still too hot to touch.

7. Place this disc or rectangle of pastry onto a tray lined with baking paper, and bake in the oven until golden brown on the top and bottom – about half an hour. Once done, leave it to cool.

8. Take care when assembling. Place your pastry upside down on a presentation plate or board, then gently turn the compressed pear out on top of it. And you've got a perfect tarte tatin without any added sugar.

# PORK WELLINGTON
MAKES ONE PORK WELLINGTON TO SERVE 6 SMALL PEOPLE OR 4 BIG ONES

The Wellington. Who really knows where its title originates from (there's very little evidence that it was named after the 1st Duke, as I believed), but I'll put it out there: who really cares? Meat and other delicious things wrapped in puff pastry? Want.

Whatever filling you're using, whether it's beef fillet, venison, salmon, pork or a vegetarian option, the principles of baking a Wellington are the same. The pastry must be properly baked on the underside, which means a combination of thin pastry, long, slow baking times and lack of soggy filling.

Which leads me back to my inevitable bugbear: the beef Wellington. To get an inside that's oozing with enough blood to indicate a non-incinerated piece of beautiful fillet, you're going to need an almightily huge, ludicrously expensive piece of meat. Or you can have raw pastry, which I can't abide.

But pork fillet? Now you're talking. The last one I got (from Waitrose, no less) was under a fiver. It's lean, healthy, and you don't risk ruining it with baking like you do with beef. For adventurers with thermometers, you're now allowed to serve it a little pink too (at 62°C).

½ x quantity puff pastry (see
    pages 202–205), or a block of
    shop-bought all-butter puff
1 large apple
150g chestnut mushrooms
1 small onion
1 sprig of thyme

1 medium pork fillet
    (about 400g)
150g black pudding
12–16 rashers of streaky bacon
sea salt and freshly ground
    black pepper
1 egg, whisked with a pinch
    of salt (egg wash)

1. Make and rest a quantity of basic puff pastry (see page 202). You'll only need half, so you can either make two Wellingtons or freeze the rest. Preheat your oven to 180°C/160°C fan/Gas 4 and line a baking tray with baking paper.

2. Peel, core and finely dice the apple, then finely dice the mushrooms and onion. Place them in a frying pan with a little oil and the thyme, and cook together on a high heat until the onions are soft and the apples have gone past the 'soft' stage and have reached the dry, caramelising stage. Set aside.

3. Score the pork fillet down its length, almost but not quite cutting it in half. Stuff with plenty of the apple mixture down its entire length. Roll the black pudding (it might be quite dry) into a long, thin sausage and place this in with the apple. Wrap your stuffed fillet tightly in streaky bacon to secure. For more flavour, you can fry your rolled-up pork in a pan on a very high heat until just browned, prior to wrapping in pastry.

4. Roll out the puff pastry into a big rectangle about the thickness of a £1 coin. The rectangle should be at least as long as your pork fillet. Then cut this into two smaller rectangles, with one about twice as wide as the other. Place the smaller rectangle onto your baking paper.

5. Place your meat on the small rectangle, with the cut edge of the pork pointing up. Brush all around the edge of the pastry with the egg wash and place the larger puff pastry rectangle on top. Press down at the sides to seal, crimping as you go. Brush all over with egg wash then score three times on top to let the steam out.

6. Bake for 45–50 minutes, or until piping hot and the top is a deep golden brown. If you have a thermometer, it should read at least 74°C in the middle if you'd like it well done. If you don't have a thermometer, gently lift the bottom and if it seems brown and crisp, it's done. Serve hot, although it's good cold, too.

# STRAWBERRY MILLE-FEUILLE

**MAKES 6 INDIVIDUAL MILLE-FEUILLES**

Mille-feuille – '1000 leaves' (though if you can make a good puff with over 1000 laminations I'll be impressed) – is another beginner-puff recipe that I believe is a great showcase for home-made puff pastry. These just don't taste as nice if you use shop-bought pastry, for that immense butteriness that derives from fresh puff is the balancing flavour here. There's no fancy trickery: there's puff, there's cream and there are strawberries.

*½ x quantity basic puff pastry*
  *(see pages 202–205)*
*300ml double cream*
*caster sugar and vanilla extract,*
  *to taste*

*1 large punnet of strawberries*
*icing sugar, for dusting*

1. Make and rest a quantity of basic puff pastry (see page 202). You'll only need half, so you can freeze the rest. Preheat your oven to 200°C/180°C/Gas 6, then line a baking tray with baking paper.

2. Roll out the puff pastry into a big square about the thickness of a £1 coin – it should be about 12 x 12 inches. Place this on the lined baking tray, prick it all over with a fork, then place another piece of baking paper on top and weight it down with a final baking tray.

3. Bake for 25–30 minutes (the latter if your baking trays are heavy), then leave to cool. Some bakers like to bake uncovered for 20 minutes, turn the pastry and then weight it down with the second tray and finish baking, but I think this is a bit of a faff and doesn't make any difference.

4. Whip the cream by hand until just coagulated, adding sugar and vanilla to taste (see page 38). Transfer to a piping bag. Chop the strawberries into manageable chunks or slices.

5. Trim the edges of your pastry with a sharp knife to make it a clean square or rectangle. Then cut it into three equal-sized rectangles.

6. Lay one on your presentation plate or board and pipe cream onto it, either in strips or blobs. Then add the chopped strawberries, either laying them out fancily or just chucking them on; I think both effects are good. Lay atop another layer of puff pastry and then add more strawberries and cream. Top with your last layer of puff and dust with icing sugar.

OPPOSITE: KIWI PAVLOVA

MERINGUE

# MERINGUE

A meringue is a light mixture made by whipping egg whites and various forms of sugar. There is a multitude of ways to present this humble mixture: it can be raw, lightly blowtorched, grilled, poached or baked to be soft, crisp, crunchy or chewy. From just egg whites and sugar. Additives merely pollute.

Magnificent meringues require good mixing and good baking. The mixing should be vigorous and long-winded and totally deprived of any fat-based products. The baking should be appropriate to the finish you are after: long and slow for crisp, standalone triumphs; fast and harsh for soft bubbliness. It may be helpful to review the 'egg' section in the Forebake chapter (see page 15).

There's a lot of hype over the difference between French meringue and Italian meringue. The former is made with plain sugar and egg whites; the latter is made by beating a hot sugar syrup into the egg whites. The Italian method makes the meringue much more stable (it doesn't deteriorate in the short term like its Gallic cousin) and is safe to eat without any further cooking. A final, less well-known method is the Swiss meringue. This involves whisking your sugar and egg whites in a bowl over a pan of simmering water (a bain marie) to pasteurise them.

The conclusion often reached is that either the Swiss or Italian meringue is better because it is more complicated. Not so. French meringue is what you want for the vast majority of bakes. You can safely eat it raw, providing you're not pregnant or immunocompromised.

This guide will take you through the French style, step by step. The alternatives will be discussed below, as I don't believe they require an entire section. They're all about whisking.

## THE IDEAL MERINGUE

The ideal baked meringue shell can be any size, from mini sweet canapés to massive towers of Pavlova discs. They should be anaemic – white to pale beige – with no sheen.

Cracks are acceptable in large meringues. There should be no 'weeping' (sugar beads) and no signs of flattening out during baking. The shell should break with a snap, causing moderate crumbling. The centre should be both light and chewy, but not so sticky as to be jaw-breaking. There should be no bitter or 'off' flavours caused by baking in an unclean oven or storing in a smelly fridge, and no background taste of cornflour, vinegar or other stabilising ancillaries. There should be no grittiness.

## BASIC FRENCH MERINGUE RECIPE
### MAKES 12 INDIVIDUAL MERINGUE SHELLS OR 6 HUGE ONES

*4 medium egg whites*
*200g caster sugar*

### LINE

Line a baking tray with baking paper. You can use a little of the meringue mixture to stick it down. Do not grease anything.

### SEPARATE

Separate the eggs (see page 117) and place the egg whites into a large glass, metal or ceramic bowl. The bowl should be clean and completely free of fat. Do not use plastic or silicone. If a yolk breaks, don't panic – use a spoon to fish any wee bits out. Shine a light into it (I use the torch on my phone) to make sure you've got it all.

### WHISK

It helps to have a stand mixer at this point; at the very least a handheld electric whisk is near-essential. Clean your beaters. Whisk your egg whites for several minutes until they're as big as they're going to get.

### WHY

Fat is the enemy of meringue. I will repeat this many times. Just have a blanket policy: when making meringues, nothing should have come into contact with any form of fat without being properly cleaned. This includes all bowls, surfaces, tools and your hands.

### WHY

Fat is the enemy of meringue. Egg whites can hold air due to their high protein content – the more you whip, the more the proteins flatten out and air is trapped between the layers. But these proteins enjoy the presence of fats a lot more than air, and will stick to them if they get a chance, bludgeoning your structure. Egg yolks are full of fat, and plastic bowls have a rough surface in which fat tends to hide. Rubbing your bowl with a little lemon juice, then drying, is a recommended extra precaution.

### WHY

Whisking the egg whites before adding the sugar is important simply to save time. You can add the sugar at this stage, but it will take ages to foam up to meringue-like levels. This is because the sugar will bind to the proteins before you've unfurled and flattened them by beating, meaning you've stabilised them in their contorted, airless state.

### BIT BY BIT

Weigh out the sugar into another bowl, removing any lumps (you might want to use a sieve, if you have one). Keep whisking on high speed, adding the sugar a teaspoon at a time, until it is all incorporated. This will take time.

### TEST

Test your meringue: make sure its peaks are stiff, and that you can hold it in a bowl above your head without any falling out. Then, if you aren't averse to it, taste the raw egg white. If there's any grittiness or sugariness, whisk for at least another couple of minutes.

### SPLODGE

Spoon or pipe your meringue onto your prepared baking paper.

### WHY

Lumps of sugar will not dissolve fully in your egg whites. If you can't crumble a lump easily with your fingers, get rid of it. 'Weeping' (beads of sugar) is often caused by insufficient dissolving of the sugar during mixing; the wee beads are usually just caramelised lumps of sugar that haven't been incorporated properly. Adding the sugar slowly is important for consistency and for aeration; you don't want to crush your delicate structure by dumping a weighty pile of sugar on top.

### WHY

Stiff peaks aren't rolling hills – they are the Alps. They should be tall and steep, harsh and stable. If you taste the meringue and it is even remotely gritty or 'sparkly' on the tongue, with tiny crystals of sugar, start whisking again – not to whip any more air in (though it can't hurt), but just to dissolve the rest of the sugar.

### WHY

If piping, you've got to be careful not to squeeze too hard through too small a hole. You want to be gentle, or this pressure could force out all the air you've incorporated through whisking.

## THE BAKE

With meringues, the bake is of prime consideration. For perfect meringue shells, slower is superior. Your oven should be preheated to a very low heat – no more than 120°C/100°C fan/Gas ½. Then you should bake your meringues for at least 1½–2 hours – feel free to open the oven door during baking, as this will aid in the drying out of the crust for a better shell. By the end, you should have minimal browning – slight beigeing, maybe. You can test whether they are baked by pressing firmly onto the shell – if it's squidgy, give it another half hour. If you poke a wee hole in it, but it's crusty, give it another 15 minutes. And if it feels hard and takes moderate pressure, it's done.

Once done, you can remove the meringues from the oven, but I find that turning off the oven and letting them cool down slowly gives a drier, crisper finish.

For a softer meringue, such as you might find in a lemon meringue pie, you want a higher heat. Meringue is very light, and so heat can penetrate easily. This means that if it is browned on a high heat, the centre cooks relatively quickly. If you'd like a thin-crusted meringue that's a glossy golden brown, crank the heat up to 180°C/160°C fan/Gas 4 and bake for 25–30 minutes.


## VARIATIONS

**SWISS MERINGUE**   This awesome, slightly spongy version of meringue is a really stable cake and pie topping, finished with a quick blowtorch or blast in a hot oven. Bring a pan of water to a simmer. Then follow the basic recipe, simply doing all the whisking with your bowl over the pan of gently simmering water. If you've got a thermometer, your meringue will be completely cooked at 70°C.

**MARSHMALLOW**   Follow the guide for Swiss meringue above, with a couple of leaves of gelatine that have been softened in water. Add them to the egg whites once they are warm and whisk in until dissolved.

**ITALIAN MERINGUE**   This stable meringue is made exactly as the French meringue, but with hot caramel rather than plain sugar. Simply take your quantity of sugar (100g per 2 egg whites) and dissolve it in a pan with water (25g per 2 egg whites). If you have a sugar thermometer, bring to a temperature of 118°C, or boil for 30 seconds if you don't. Then, slowly whisk this syrup into your stiff egg whites.

**CHOCOLATE MERINGUE**   Chocolate meringue, dipped in chocolate, with a chocolate cream or ganache filling works very well. And it's simple: fold in a heaped teaspoon of unsweetened cocoa powder to your finished meringue for every egg white you've used. It's an idea to sieve the cocoa, as it needs to be well incorporated for a nice finish.

**ADJUNCT MERINGUE**   For a swirly, fancy-looking meringue, mix any form of extract or flavouring with an appropriate food colouring, then lightly fold this in at the end to make swirls. For example, mix pink food colouring with rosewater, or yellow food colouring with lemon zest. Equally, you could just fold in some vanilla, chocolate or almond extract for a kick.

**NUTTY MERINGUE**   It's common to make meringue shells with chopped nuts sprinkled on top before baking. If doing this, don't use a food processor; instead, chop the nuts finely by hand. Being too aggressive with them will release their oils and make your meringues collapse underneath them. My favourites are pistachios and blanched hazelnuts.

## SUBSTITUTIONS

**EGGS**   There aren't very many substitutions you can make in a meringue. One common one, however, that means you don't need to go to the bother of making a Swiss or Italian meringue but still have topping that is 'safe' for all to eat, is to use pasteurised egg whites. Use about 35g in place of each egg white.

**VEGAN**   Meringues are pretty good for people who can't eat certain food groups, but vegans will have to suffer on. Vegan meringues are possible using a mixture of soya protein, vinegar and xanthan gum, but I've tried them and they aren't very good. Googling will find you plenty of quite poor recipes.

## STORAGE

Meringues can be stored in their raw state in the fridge for a few hours, max. But Italian or Swiss meringues will keep 'stable' for up to two days in the fridge, depending on the humidity.

Baked meringue will keep relatively well in an airtight container at room temperature for a good few days. But if making them in advance, I'd recommend freezing them in a freezer bag or airtight container. They freeze excellently, so when defrosted tend to be just as good as when they came out the oven. Be careful not to damage any beautiful peaks or swirls when storing.

## TROUBLESHOOTING

*Why are there beads of sugar on my baked meringues?* This is called 'weeping' and occurs as a result of wee pockets of sugar collecting in your meringue, attracting water and then caramelising. This can be a result of rapid baking in an oven that's too hot, adding your sugar too quickly, adding sugar in lumps, or simply adding too much sugar. Make sure your oven is on a very low heat, and once you've added your sugar keep whisking for several more minutes to make sure everything is combined.

*Why won't my meringues form stiff peaks?* Meringues and fat don't mix. Therefore, this could be due to an unclean mixing bowl (don't use plastic or silicone), or perhaps you left a bit of yolk in with the egg whites. If you're certain this isn't the case, try getting some fresh eggs. Although some pâtissiers prefer to use old eggs, their degraded protein structure can cause difficulties.

*Why did my meringues flatten out in the oven?* The fact is, even if you have a bit of fat in your mix, your meringues can still form stiff peaks. But if you then bake them, they don't have the structure to stay as they were. Make sure you've got a clean bowl (no plastic or silicone) and no trace of yolk in it. If still no luck, use fresh eggs and beat in the sugar very slowly.

*Why do my meringues shrink?* The most likely explanation is that your meringue had a high water content, which then evaporated in the oven. This could be due to making meringue on a humid day. It could also be down to not using enough sugar, or it could be that you baked Italian meringue, which does shrink.

*Why are my meringues chewy and take ages to bake?* Again, this is due to a high water content, but most people don't mind it in my experience. At home, it is usually a result of high humidity, which is difficult to solve. To compensate, try upping the sugar by a few teaspoons.

# ROSE MERINGUE KISSES
### MAKES 36 SMALL KISSES

Valentine's day coming up? An anniversary? You could make this recipe. Or you could leave this page open in an obvious place and hope your other half gets the idea. If it comes to the big day and you're meringueless, it's probably time to end it.

   This recipe is also appropriate for post-breakup consolation. *(Pictured overleaf.)*

*4 medium egg whites*
*200g caster sugar*
*1 teaspoon rosewater*

*concentrated red or pink food*
*colouring (artificial gels,*
*not natural)*

1. Preheat your oven to 120°C/100°C fan/Gas ½.

2. Into a large, clean bowl (not plastic or silicone), place the egg whites. They should be free of any trace of yolk – if there is any remaining, use a spoon to scoop it out and use a torch or the light on your phone to make sure there's none left.

3. Using an electric whisk or stand mixer on the highest speed available, whisk the whites until light, fluffy and stiff. When they're not getting any bigger, start adding the caster sugar, a teaspoon at a time, still whisking on the highest speed. When it's all incorporated, keep whisking for a bit longer before setting aside.

4. Prepare a large piping bag for the kisses. First, turn the bag inside out and stand it up like a cone, using a bottle of wine to stabilise it. Then, mix the rosewater with a little food colouring in a wee cup. Using a brush, paint this mixture in four or five stripes down the inside of your piping bag (which is the outside right now, because it's inside out).

5. Place your hand inside the cone (where the wine bottle was). Scoop all your glossy meringue mixture into the piping bag, using your hand to 'grab' it from the other side of the bag, until all your mix is in there. Give the bag a wee roll around and a bash to mix the colouring with the meringue.

6. Cut a 1.5–2cm hole in the end of your bag, then pipe four wee corners onto a baking tray and use them to stick a piece of baking paper down to line the tray. Now, pipe your kisses onto the baking paper – pipe a blob, then lift the bag gradually to create a peak. You'll improve as you go along.

7. Bake your meringues for about an hour, until they've dried out completely. Check them after 40 minutes or so, just to make sure they're not colouring. If any of them are, turn your oven down as low as it will go. I would suggest serving with fresh lychees and rose petals…

# KIWI PAVLOVA
## MAKES ONE SIZEABLE SPECTACLE

In my short life, there have been a few individuals and associated bakes that have sparked my passion for baking. I talked loads about my gran in my first book and in pretty much every interview I've ever done. But one person I've never mentioned is Mike Skinner. When I was wee, but sometime after I was beginning to feel too cool to bake cakes, my dad would take me to the café Mike ran, usually after my Saturday morning rollerblading session (my sole exercise of the week).

Despite Shetland's tradition for sensational home-baking, this was the only place that would do it on demand. The muffins were good, but the Pavlova was excellent. My favourite contained only kiwi, the green juice pooling between the never-ending waves of whipped cream. There would be an attempt to slice it, but then it would simply be scraped from its tray and shovelled into a bowl. Just as it should be. Thank you, Mike.

This is basic and I am not sorry. You can use any fruit, though kiwi is best. Do not use a piping bag. Do not glaze. (Pictured overleaf.)

| | |
|---|---|
| 4 medium egg whites | caster sugar and vanilla extract, |
| 200g caster sugar | to taste |
| 1 pint double cream | 6 kiwi fruits |

1. First, preheat your oven to 120°C/100°C fan/Gas ½.

2. Into a large, clean bowl (not plastic or silicone), place the egg whites. They should be free of any trace of yolk – if there is any remaining, use a spoon to scoop it out and use a torch or the light on your phone to make sure there's none left.

3. Using an electric whisk or stand mixer on the highest speed available, whisk the whites until light, fluffy and stiff. When they're not getting any bigger, start adding the caster sugar, a teaspoon at a time, still whisking on the highest speed. When it's all incorporated, keep whisking for a bit longer before setting aside.

4. Use a wee touch of the meringue to stick a sheet of baking paper to a baking tray. Then, scoop your meringue into one massive circular blob. Try to make it thinner in the middle and thicker towards the edges. A thicker crust is required because so much of the centre will become soggy when laden with cream.

5. Bake your meringue for approximately 2 hours – I like a bit of beige (even brown) on my Pavlova. Leave it to cool on the tray.

6. Whip the cream by hand in a cold bowl until just coagulated, adding sugar and vanilla to taste (see my guide on page 38). Peel and slice the kiwi fruits.

7. Scoop about half the cream on top of the meringue disc and spread it around. Add about a third of the kiwi fruits then cover completely with another layer of cream and top with the rest of the fruit. Preferably in a big pile. Keep in the fridge and serve over the course of the following day.

# ÎLES FLOTTANTES
## MAKES SIX ÎLES FLOTTANTES

Îles flottantes – 'floating islands' – are poached rather than baked meringues. They're served at room temperature or cold with crème anglaise for some serious goo on goo action. They might sound awful if you've never had them before, but trust me. They. Are. Sublime.

Some people like to retain the poaching liquor to make the custard, and you can try this if you're thrifty. But I don't believe this is conducive to having a life. I will make the custard in advance if I have time, or I'll buy it from Waitrose. And if you're not planning on reusing it, you can add flavours: vanilla and almond extracts are both scrummy. *(Pictured overleaf.)*

*1 x quantity crème anglaise*
  *(see page 24)*
*booze, to mix into the*
  *crème anglaise, optional*
*2 medium egg whites*
*100g caster sugar*
*1 pint whole milk*

*For the praline*
*100g flaked, roasted almonds*
  *(roast in a 200°C oven for*
  *5 minutes)*
*100g caster sugar*
*1 tablespoon water*

1. First, make the crème anglaise (see page 24). Mix your favourite booze in at the end if desired, then leave it in the fridge to chill. Because warm custard is for cold-hearted people.

2. Next, make the praline. Place the almonds on a sheet of baking paper, and the sugar and water in a pan. Place the pan on a medium heat, stirring until the sugar has dissolved. Stop stirring. Boil until the mixture turns a deep dark brown (see my guide on pages 27 and 69). Pour this over the almonds.

3. Pour the milk into a large frying pan, place on a low heat and slowly bring to a simmer. Whilst you do that, make the meringue.

4. Into a large, clean bowl (not plastic or silicone), place the egg whites. They should be free of any trace of yolk – if there is any remaining, use a spoon to scoop it out and use a torch or the light on your phone to make sure there's none left.

5. Using an electric whisk or stand mixer on the highest speed available, whisk the whites until light, fluffy and stiff. When they're not getting any bigger, start adding the caster sugar, a teaspoon at a time, still whisking on the highest speed. When it's all incorporated, keep whisking for a bit longer.

6. Scoop six lumps of the meringue into the simmering pan of milk – I think the rougher looking the better in this dish. But maybe that's just me. Turn regularly – they're done when they are big and puffy and feel slightly bouncy when pressed. It'll take about 10 minutes.

7. Once done, place on a piece of kitchen paper or a rack to dry out slightly, then chill until needed.

8. To assemble, make a pool of cold crème Anglaise on a plate. Pop a meringue into the centre of the pool, then smash your almond praline into bits and scatter on top. Simple.

# MANGO, RASPBERRY & PISTACHIO ROULADE

MAKES ONE LARGE ROULADE

Rolled-up meringue. What's not amazing about that?

My favourite thing about this dish is that I have no Swiss roll tin. I use a small roasting tray, cover it in a double layer of foil with plenty sticking out over the ends, then I grease it with a little butter at the sides and cut out a square of baking paper to go over the bottom. It makes me feel like I'm sticking it to all those respectable vendors of apparent kitchen necessities whenever I walk down the baking aisle and don't buy a Swiss roll tin. Which is often.

100g unsalted pistachios,
    shelled
4 medium egg whites
200g caster sugar

300ml double cream
caster sugar, to taste
flesh of 2 mangoes
1 punnet of fresh raspberries

1. First, preheat your oven to 200°C/180°C fan/Gas 6. Prepare your intricate roasting-tray arrangement in place of a Swiss roll tin (see the introduction above). Unless you actually have a Swiss roll tin, in which case use it. Grind the pistachios in a food processor (or crush them by hand) until a mixture of powder and lumps.

2. Into a large, clean bowl (not plastic or silicone), place the egg whites. They should be free of any trace of yolk – if there is any remaining, use a spoon to scoop it out and use a torch or the light on your phone to make sure there's none left.

3. Using an electric whisk or stand mixer on the highest speed available, whisk the whites until light, fluffy and stiff. When they're not getting any bigger, start adding the caster sugar, a teaspoon at a time, still whisking on the highest speed. When it's all incorporated, keep whisking for a bit longer.

4. Spread the meringue out to cover the tin and sprinkle most of your pistachios on top. Bake for 10 minutes at this high temperature to brown them, then reduce the oven temperature to 150°C/130°C fan/Gas 2 and bake for another 20 minutes in order to firm up.

5. When it is done, remove the meringue from the tin/foil and turn it onto a sheet of baking paper or cling film, so that the pistachio side is on the bottom. Remove the paper that it was baked on and allow it to cool whilst you prepare the filling.

6. Whip the cream by hand in a cold bowl until just coagulated, adding sugar to taste (see page 38). In a blender or food processor, blend your mango flesh to a purée. Again, add sugar to taste. Press your raspberries through a sieve into another bowl. Yet again, add sugar to taste.

7. Spread your cream over the meringue and then sprinkle the rest of your pistachios on top. Splash your mango and raspberry purées over the top, Jackson Pollock-style. Roll up the roulade, using the paper to help you. You should roll it as tight as you can. I like to think those cracks look quite rustic.

8. You could also make a syrup for drizzling by placing the remaining mango purée in a pan on a high heat and reducing it down. This is worth it just for the smell in the kitchen. Serve with dollops of the remaining cream and drizzles of the syrup.

MACARON

# MACARON

A macaron is a French confection usually made of two layers of crisp, almondy meringue and a flavoured filling of contrasting texture in the middle. They have come into fashion in a big way and may soon be set for ceremonious abandonment alongside precariously iced cupcakes and mouth-welding cake-pops. But my instinct tells me that would be a terrible shame, for macarons have finally added substance to that pretentious discord of pretty wee treats.

Although they have a reputation for trickiness, I believe this results from a consistent lack of proper instruction. The key is to break things down into lots of short step-by-steps – each step is essential and any haste or deviation can be disastrous. Follow my instructions and you'll get perfect rounds of pure pleasure every time.

Macarons are often referred to as 'macaroons', and I don't despise this, but I do feel it confuses matters. Macarons are in no way similar to the super-sweet, chewy, coconut-based macaroons. They deserve better.

## THE IDEAL MACARON

The perfect macaron base can be any size, from 1cm to 30cm wide or more. Even the height can vary, depending on the consistency of the macaron mix and what result is sought. For a thicker, dome-like macaron, don't beat as much air out of your mixture during the final mixing. For a thinner, more biscuity macaron, keep beating your final mix until it flows in smooth ribbons.

They can be any colour too, usually achieved through artificial means. One thing that must be present, however, is the 'foot' (*le pied*, as the French say): the ruffled-looking bit around the edge that appears as a result of the rise in the oven.

The top of the macaron should be smooth, and may be matt or shiny. It commonly features sprinkles, glitter or flavoured sugar to add distinction in taste, texture or appearance. It should not brown in the oven.

Macarons are typically presented with two shells and a filling sandwiched in between. The filling can be created from almost anything, but it should be soft so as to impart flavour into the shells. A desirable macaron has a gentle crunch at the surface and a soft-but-not-gooey centre, depending on the filling chosen.

## BASIC MACARON SHELLS RECIPE
### MAKES ABOUT 24 SIZEABLE (2.5–4CM) SHELLS FOR 12 ASSEMBLED MACARONS

*100g icing sugar*
*60g ground almonds*
*2 medium egg whites*
*40g caster sugar*
*a dash of food colouring, preferably gel-based*

### BLITZ
First, weigh out the icing sugar and almonds, then use a food processor or stick blender to grind them together. If grinding facilities are unavailable, at least sieve them.

### WHY
Grinding gets rid of lumps and combines your ingredients. It may also achieve an extra-fine grind on your almonds, though the importance of this is overstated.

### WHISK
Put the egg whites into a large glass or stainless-steel bowl (not plastic), and whisk until they hold their shape in stiff peaks.

### WHY
You are whisking air into the egg whites – this will expand in the oven to give a lightness to your macarons.

### SUGAR
Add the caster sugar to the egg whites, a teaspoon at a time, whisking in between each addition. Keep going until it is all incorporated.

### WHY
You need to add the sugar slowly to give each spoonful a chance to dissolve fully in the mix. Any undissolved grains of sugar will melt into a caramel and 'weep' (like little tears), and will give your macarons an uneven, gritty texture.

### COLOUR

Add the food colouring and about half the almondy icing sugar mixture to the egg whites and slowly fold this into your mix until combined. Add more food colouring if required.

### WHY

Adding it in two batches makes it easier to incorporate the almond mix, and evens out the colour.

### LAVA

Add the rest of the almondy icing sugar and mix everything together, gently but sternly enough to bash some of the air out. Keep going until the mix flows slowly from the spoon. It should be the exact consistency of lava flowing down the side of a volcano (if unsure, search YouTube for 'lava volcano').

### WHY

Macarons are not meringues; you bash the air out to stop them rising too much in the oven and to allow a glossy skin to form on top. Go too far, though, and you won't get good 'feet' and your mix will spread out all over your tray.

### PIPE

Fill a piping bag with your mix and cut a 1cm hole in the end. Line a thin baking tray with non-stick baking paper (use little dots of macaron mix to stick your paper to your tray), then pipe little blobs of mix onto the tray. These should be about two-thirds of the diameter of your final macaron shells. Some people like to use a template or draw circles to help them achieve a consistent size. I don't.

### WHY

Piping is pretty essential to achieve the exact round shape you're going for, and for consistency in size, though you can use a spoon if you want to. It is important to bake on as thin a baking tray as you have, so the heat can penetrate from all sides. If you use non-stick baking paper you won't have to grease the tray and get fat into your macarons, which would disturb the structure. Avoid silicone mats; they tend to absorb grease and many don't prevent sticking.

### DROP

Lift your tray at least a foot or two above your work surface and then let it go to smash down. Repeat twice more.

### REST

ESSENTIAL: Leave your macarons uncovered at room temperature for at least half an hour before baking. The longer the better.

### WHY

This isn't just for dramatic effect – it pops any of the bigger, more fragile bubbles within your macarons and spreads them out slightly on your tray. This gives them a more even rise in the oven with a smoother finish.

### WHY

This is *the most important step*. It allows the surface of the macarons to dry out and a skin to form. This means that when you bake, the surface stays intact and your macarons only rise from the bottom upwards, giving you perfect 'feet'.

## THE BAKE

The macaron's bake is an issue that divides pâtissières the world over. One thing is agreed: they should receive as little additional colour as possible whilst in the oven. This doesn't mean that your final macarons will be exactly the same colour as your mix. They won't – they'll be ever so slightly 'beige-ified'. But they should not be baked to the point at which they are becoming golden.

For 'normal-sized' macarons (about 2.5–4cm wide), I bake at 170°C/150°C fan/Gas 3 for 12 minutes, quickly opening and then closing the oven twice during baking (at about 6 and 9 minutes). Opening the oven isn't essential, but it lets out any steam and makes the surface of the macarons ever-so-slightly crisper. For tiny petit fours, reduce the time to 9 minutes and up the temperature by about 10°C.

If you're making larger macarons, you'll need to bake for longer at a lower temperature – I recommend 160°C/140°C fan/Gas 3, with regular checking. You'll want to give them at least 15–18 minutes. If you bake them so they are crisp all the way through, don't fret. As they absorb their filling, they'll soften up on the inside. And if you've really gone too far, spray them lightly with some water from a spray bottle.

For a great shine on the surface and to ensure that the flavours of the filling are properly absorbed into the shell, chill the macarons in the fridge at least overnight. Make sure you keep them away from anything with a strong odour because the porous shells absorb all aromas.

If you're serving your macarons the same day, freeze the shells for half an hour before you assemble them. Freezing does not affect their flavour.


## VARIATIONS

ITALIAN MERINGUE MACARONS   For years, this was all I made. Rather than whisking caster sugar into your mix, you make a sugar syrup and whisk that in instead. This basically cooks the egg whites and makes the meringue much more stable and therefore much more forgiving. Without good instruction, I had many fails with French meringue macarons before my first success with Italian. To make an Italian meringue macaron mix, use the basic recipe but reduce the icing sugar to 60g. Up the caster sugar to 80g, but instead of incorporating it into your egg whites, bring it to the boil in a pan with 25g of water. Keep boiling until the temperature reaches 118°C on a sugar thermometer – this is the 'soft ball' stage. Whisking all the time, pour the sugar syrup slowly into your puffy egg whites, then continue as above.

CARAMEL   Make an Italian meringue as above, but when making the syrup, boil it until it turns a deep, dark caramel colour. Then cool until nearly set, add 40g water, return to the heat and boil again until it reaches 118°C. Whisking all the time, pour the caramel slowly into your puffy egg whites.

**GLITTER/SUGAR** Many macaron variants are purely aesthetic. There are plenty of glitters and sprays available, but just mixing caster sugar with food colouring makes a nice sparkly effect (sprinkle onto the shells just before baking). To add subtle hints of aromatic flavours, mix an ingredient of your choice into the coloured sugar. Adding a chopped fresh chilli in this way adds a bit of heat to chocolate or lime macarons, for example.

**SIZE** A macaron doesn't have to be wee and delicate. Make your mix of quite a thick consistency, then pipe in a spiral to make a large macaron disc. This can be used to make magnificent layered desserts or as a great gluten-free alternative to a celebration cake.

## SUBSTITUTIONS

**NUTS** One of the most interesting and useful substitutions involves replacing the almonds with another ingredient. Macarons will work with any ground nuts – pistachios and hazelnuts are particularly good. Many nuts are not widely available in ground form, so you'll need a food processor or a good blender for this. Walnuts are great for making savoury macarons. For totally nut-free macarons, try replacing with finely grated white chocolate.

**EGG WHITES** You can replace the two medium egg whites with 70g of pasteurised egg white. And vegans can enjoy macarons too: mix 60g of water with 15g of egg replacer powder and ¼ teaspoon of xanthan gum and use as egg whites above.

**SUGAR** Oh, just get a grip, you sugar haters! Each tiny macaron shell has minimal sugar in it. Want to eat less sugar? Eat one less macaron, or go for a savoury filling.

## STORAGE

Macarons should be stored in the fridge in an airtight container and can be enjoyed for up to five days after baking. Of course, if you've used a perishable ingredient such as cream as a filling, go by the use-by date of the cream.

Macarons freeze particularly well. You can store the baked, unfilled shells in an airtight container in the freezer for up to six months. They can then be assembled straight from frozen. Or if you've already filled them with fillings that aren't all that moist (ganache or buttercream), you can freeze them whole. Defrost for 30–45 minutes before serving.

## TROUBLESHOOTING

*Why don't my macarons have 'feet'?* The most common macaron issue is usually responsible here: you haven't left them to rest for long enough before baking. If you followed the guide above and they're still wrong, it's probably because your oven temperature is a little too high.

*Why don't my macarons have a smooth surface?* There could be two problems here. The first is that your egg whites are too big – make sure they are medium eggs (or weigh out 35g white per egg). The other possibility is that you didn't beat enough air out when doing the final mix.

*Why do my macarons taste awful?* Clean your oven. Macarons absorb all the aromas they are exposed to, especially during the bake. My first ever batch all those years ago tasted like porky fish because that's what we'd been cooking the nights before.

*Why are my macarons sticking?* Make sure you are using baking parchment (non-stick greaseproof paper). Some silicone mats work, some don't. The other possibility is that your macarons are underbaked – they will lift off easily when properly baked.

*Why do my macarons splay out when I leave them to rest?* You could have beaten your mix too much before piping, but do also check the size of your eggs. Make sure they're medium.

*Why do my macarons have little peaks on top?* This is down to your piping. Once you've piped your splodge onto the paper, press down into the splodge before lifting your bag up straight. And make sure your mix is slack enough (just mix it a little more).

# BLACKBERRY TART MACARON

MAKES 4–6 MACARONS (8–12 SHELLS), DEPENDING ON SIZE

As a stand-alone dessert, this recipe is unusual. Macarons are not usually desserts – they can sometimes be *on* desserts so the pompous creator (myself included) can show off a bit. But on their own they are petit fours or individual treats, too small to be a proper pudding.

These are massive bruisers of macarons, however, designed to be demolished as individual desserts to round off a meal in the most elaborate way possible.

Except it's actually a con because this is dead easy. Follow the basic macaron recipe, then all that's needed is a simple and very soft cream cheese icing and some blackberries.

And the best thing about macarons as a dessert? They get better with a bit of 'ageing' in the fridge, so you can make these the night before.

100g icing sugar
60g ground almonds
2 medium egg whites
40g caster sugar
dark purple food colouring
    (or a mix of blue and red)

**For the filling**
150g cream cheese
    (must be full-fat and chilled)
150g icing sugar

a bunch of fresh mint,
    finely chopped
finely grated zest of 1 lime
3 punnets of fresh blackberries

**For the glaze (optional)**
a handful of blackberries (from
    the 3 punnets used for the
    filling)
3 tablespoons caster sugar

1. Line a baking tray with a piece of baking paper. In a food processor or blender, blitz together the icing sugar and almonds to remove any lumps.

2. In a large glass or stainless-steel bowl, whisk your egg whites to stiff peaks. Add the caster sugar, a teaspoon at a time, whisking on the highest speed (if using an electric mixer) all the time. Once your sugar is incorporated, whisk in enough food colouring to take it to a colour you like.

3. Fold in half your almondy mix as carefully as you can. Then add the final half and gently beat out a little of the air to loosen the mix. It should flow from the spoon like lava down the side of a mountain.

4. Fill a piping bag with your mix, cut a 1cm hole in the end and pipe 8–12 big splodges or spirals onto the baking paper, about 4-6cm in width, so that when they splay out slightly they will be up to 8cm in diameter. Pick up the tray and drop it from 1-2 feet onto the work surface. Do this twice more to remove any big bubbles.

5. Leave the macarons to rest for 30 minutes *at the very least,* for the skins to form, so they don't split in the oven.

6. Whilst the skins are forming, preheat your oven to 160°C/140°C fan/Gas 3, then prepare your cream cheese filling. Simply whisk the cream cheese and icing sugar together with an electric mixer on a high speed (or by hand with a lot of effort) – when the mix is thick and creamy, keep going; you can incorporate air like whipping cream. Stir in the mint and lime zest, adjusting to taste. Scoop the filling into another piping bag.

7. Make your glaze, if desired. Take 5 or 6 blackberries in a bowl and crush them with the back of a spoon. Pour the juice into a pan and add a tablespoon of water and the caster sugar. Bring the mixture to the boil over a high heat then set aside, off the heat, until needed.

8. Bake your macarons for about 15–18 minutes, or until 'feet' have formed, they feel crisp to touch, but have not yet coloured. Leave them to cool on the tray.

9. To build, make a circle of blackberries around the outside of the underside of a cooled shell (you can use a touch of the icing if they keep falling down). Then, pipe a generous amount of your icing inside, closing with another macaron shell. To finish, brush all visible fruit with a little glaze.

# HAZELNUT, LEMON & RASPBERRY MACARONS

MAKES 12 MACARONS

If you want a recipe to impress, this has to be it. It may seem quite tricky at first glance, but look a little closer and you'll see it's just some standard macaron shells, a simple white chocolate ganache and jam.

My first iteration of these macarons was based on the lime, chilli and raspberry macarons I created to clone a memory from Paris. I made them on *The Great British Bake Off* to rave reviews and a star-bakership, but I still wasn't happy with them.

The lime and raspberry worked great, but I felt that the chilli didn't quite gel with the whole thing.

This was remedied with a little experimentation. The shells themselves are now made in the normal way, but with ground hazelnuts instead of almonds. The white chocolate ganache in the filling has extra lemon to cut through any richness. And finally, the centre is just raspberry jam, and all the better for it. This is an evidence-based, molecularly sound flavour combination and, quite simply, awesome.

*100g icing sugar*
*60g ground hazelnuts*
*2 medium egg whites*
*40g caster sugar*
*a few extra hazelnuts, chopped,*
  *for decoration*

*For the filling*
*150g white chocolate*
*25g salted butter*
*50g lemon juice*
*high-quality raspberry jam*

1. Line a baking tray with baking paper. In a food processor or blender, grind together the icing sugar and hazelnuts until fine.

2. In a large glass or stainless-steel bowl, whisk the egg whites to stiff peaks. Add the sugar, a teaspoon at a time, whisking after each addition.

3. Add half your hazelnutty mixture and fold together gently. Add the other half and mix, beating some of the air out, until it flows slowly from your spoon, like lava down the side of a mountain.

4. Fill a piping bag with your mix, cut a 1cm hole in the end, and pipe 24 blobs onto the baking paper, so that when they splay out slightly they will be about 2.5–4cm in diameter. Pick up the tray and drop it from several feet onto the work surface. Do this twice more to remove any big bubbles.

5. Leave your macarons uncovered for 30 minutes *at the very least* to allow a skin to form.

6. Whilst the skins are forming, preheat your oven to 170°C/150°C fan/Gas 3, then prepare your ganache. Melt the chocolate and butter together in a microwave, or in a bowl over a pan of

simmering water, as slowly as you can. When it's liquid, add the lemon juice and quickly mix everything together until smooth. Place this in a piping bag, ready to use later. If it's cold in your house and it hardens up, a quick blast in the microwave when you're ready to use it will fix it.

7. Sprinkle the chopped hazelnuts over your rested shells and bake for 12 minutes, opening the oven door twice during the bake to let the steam out. When they're done, leave them to cool on the tray until they reach room temperature.

8. Cut a 0.5cm hole in your ganache piping bag, then pipe onto the underside of a macaron shell in a ring shape. Place a splodge of raspberry jam into the hole in the centre. Place another macaron shell on top and repeat with the remaining shells.

# ORANGE BLOSSOM & CREAM CHEESE
## MACARONS
MAKES 12 MACARONS

I got this idea from one of the limited, exclusive releases by world-renowned macaron master, Pierre Herme. I was fascinated by his use of 'cream cheese' as a listed flavour in his recipes, and thought I'd try it. My favourite thing about this recipe is that it isn't that sweet; in fact, you can just eat more and more and you always want another. Dangerous.

I found that simple was best, using orange blossom as the main flavour component to match with sharp cream cheese. If you would like another dimension, make a passion fruit jelly by boiling sieved passion fruit juice, a leaf of gelatine and a touch of sugar. Cut this into blocks and place in the middle as a little surprise. Alternatively, drizzle a little orange or lemon curd into the middle of your filling.

100g icing sugar
60g ground almonds
2 medium egg whites
40g caster sugar
orange food colouring

**For the filling**
½ x quantity of crème pat
  (see page 23)
a little orange or
  lemon curd (see page 36),
  optional
150g cream cheese, full-fat and
  chilled
1 teaspoon orange
  flower water

1. Line a baking tray with baking paper. In a food processor or blender, grind together the icing sugar and almonds until fine.

2. In a large glass or stainless-steel bowl, whisk the egg whites to stiff peaks. Add the caster sugar, a teaspoon at a time, whisking after each addition.

3. Add half your almondy mixture and fold everything together gently. Add the other half and mix, beating enough of the air out so that it flows slowly from your spoon. It should be the exact consistency of lava running down the side of a mountain.

4. Fill a piping bag with your mix, cut a 1cm hole in the end, and pipe 24 blobs onto the baking paper, so that when they splay out slightly they will be about 2.5–4cm in diameter. Pick up the tray and drop it from several feet onto the work surface. Do this twice more to remove any big bubbles.

5. Leave your macarons uncovered for 30 minutes *at the very least*, to allow a skin to form.

6. Whilst the skins are forming, preheat your oven to 170°C/150°C fan/Gas 3, then prepare your crème pat (see page 23). Place it in the freezer to cool quicker. You can also make the curd now (see page 36) if you'd like to add a wee surprise into the middle of your macarons.

7. Bake your macarons for 10–12 minutes, opening the oven door twice during the bake to let the steam out. When they're done, leave them to cool on the tray until they reach room temperature.

8. Once the crème pat is cool, beat it into your cream cheese and orange flower water until silky and smooth. Then fill a piping bag fitted with a star nozzle and pipe a ring shape onto the underside of one shell, drizzling a little orange or lemon curd into the middle if desired and then sandwiching with another layer. Repeat with the remaining shells.

# CARAMEL MACARONS

MAKES 12 MACARONS

I've been thinking – how can you make a caramel macaron more caramelly? Why stop at just stuffing it with caramel? Messy fingers was all I could come up with as a reason not to cover the shell itself in sticky deliciousness. But that has never stopped me before. The magnificence of these macarons is great to behold, and the caramel will cover a multitude of macaron sins, but you need to be careful when handling them – fingerprints are very noticeable.

See my guide to caramel on page 27 for how to create spun sugar and other fancy things. If you don't want sticky fingers, you could add a disc of caramel inside instead.

And for those with confidence in their ability, follow my suggestion for caramel shells in the Variations (see page 240). *(Pictured overleaf.)*

*100g icing sugar*
*60g ground almonds*
*2 medium egg whites*
*40g caster sugar*

*For the topping, optional*
*200g caster sugar*
*1 tablespoon water*

*For the filling*
*175g caster sugar*
*125g double cream*
*175g softened, unsalted butter*
*1 teaspoon flaked sea salt*

1. Line a baking tray with baking paper. Then make the caramel filling. You'll need two pans. Into one, place the caster sugar with a tablespoon or so of water. Place this over a high heat and stir until the sugar has dissolved. Then stop stirring and heat until a glorious deep, dark brown. If you have any trouble, see my guide to caramel on page 27.

2. Whilst that's heating, place the cream in the second pan and bring to the boil gradually over a medium heat, stirring occasionally. Once the caramel has reached its desired colour, remove it from the heat to stop it bubbling and add the boiling cream, stirring all the time. Leave to cool whilst you make the macaron mix.

3. In a food processor or blender, grind together the icing sugar and almonds until fine. In a large glass or stainless-steel bowl, whisk your egg whites to stiff peaks. Add the sugar, a teaspoon at a time, whisking after each addition.

4. Add half your almondy mixture and fold together gently. Add the other half and mix, beating some of the air out, until it flows slowly from your spoon, like lava oozing down the side of a mountain.

5.  Fill a piping bag with your mix, cut a 1cm hole in the end, and pipe about 24 blobs onto baking paper, so that when they splay out slightly they will be about 2.5–4cm in diameter. Pick up the tray and drop it from several feet onto the work surface. Do this twice more, to remove any big bubbles. Leave your macarons uncovered for 30 minutes *at the very least*, to allow a skin to form.

6.  Whilst the skins are forming, preheat your oven to 170°C/150°C fan/Gas 3, then finish the caramel. Dice the softened butter into chunks and add this to the caramel along with the salt. Stir vigorously. If your caramel has hardened too much, put it in the microwave and give it a quick zap.

7.  Bake your macarons for 10–12 minutes, opening the oven door twice during the bake to let the steam out. When they're done, leave them to cool on the tray until they reach room temperature.

8.  Scoop your caramel filling into a piping bag (again, heat gently to soften if it's too hard to pipe). Cut a 0.5cm hole in the end and pipe a generous layer of caramel onto the centre of the underside of one shell. Place another macaron shell on top to squish.

9.  Finally, for an extra flourish, make a caramel topping by dissolving the caster sugar in a tablespoon of water in a pan over a high heat. Continue bubbling until dark then remove from the heat. Once cooled to a kind of gooey consistency, dip one side of your macaron into it and then slowly remove. Otherwise, make wee spun sugar nests for the top (see page 27), or if you made tiny macarons, try coating them completely in caramel then fishing them out with a spoon.

INDEX

# INDEX

THIS BOOK IS BECAUSE OF MY GRANNY, AUDREY BOWIE.

BUT IT COULDN'T HAVE BEEN WRITTEN WITHOUT THE
SUPPORT, LOVE AND DRIVE PROVIDED BY FENELLA.

THE PEOPLE YOU'VE GOT TO THANK FOR ACTUALLY MAKING
THIS BOOK ACTUALLY GOOD, THOUGH, ARE:

SARAH LAVELLE, THE BEST AND LOVELIEST EDITOR THE WORLD WILL EVER SEE;

ANDY SEWELL, AN INSPIRATIONAL, EXQUISITE PHOTOGRAPHER;

WILL WEBB, A DESIGNER DEFINITELY WORTH EMPLOYING AS AN ART DIRECTOR;

TIM HAYWARD, HOST-EXTRAORDINAIRE AND ALL-ROUND TOP BLOKE;

AL, LIB, JENNI, CHRISTINA, JAMES, ELLIOTT AND TILLY FOR ALL THEIR
HELP DURING THE SHOOTS. TILL NEXT TIME?

AS ALWAYS, MY FAMILY AND FRIENDS: MUM, DAD, MARTHA, MAGNUS, DAVE (AND FAMILY),
SANDY (AND FAMILY), AUNT JANE, PAUL, HANNAH, OWEN, PAUL, SARAH, RICH, JULIA, ISLA,
CLAIRE AND CATHRYN. ALL OF YOU WERE THERE IN PERSON OR IN SPIRIT.

CHEERS TO ALL AT EBURY FOR PUBLISHING ME (AGAIN – THANKS, GUYS),
STUART FOR ASKING THEM TO AND LAURA HIGGINSON FOR PICKING UP THE PIECES.
CHEERS TO KIN FOR INTRODUCING ME TO SHARP THINGS.